Introdu 2.
SLC or b_____Page 13.
Three months too long_____Page 27.
Abigai_____Page 54.
Lonely decision time_____Page 67.
Haley_____Page 77.
Beginning of summer, 2015__Page 98.
Mid-summer, 2015_____Page 109.
End of summer, 2015_____Page 121.
Money speaks in Utah.- Robert Redford
_____Page 136.
September 30,2014 to September 29, 2015_____Page 154.
End_____Page 171.
Instagram/twitter: jonespaaron
Email: ap.jones2012@gmail.com

Dedicated to Justen Hundley, Jared Hinton, Jonathan Fuller, Daylynn Lingerfelt, Miranda Morgan and Branton Bradford
Without their successes, I would not have felt compelled to seek and make my own.

Introduction

My intention with the effort of detailing my first year while residing in Salt Lake city is not to boast or be arrogant in any way shape or form. My intention instead is to show the inner and outer struggles of making drastic changes in one's life. The following memoir is about my life in Salt Lake City in chronological order from September 29,2014 to September 29, 2015.

My goal with this book is to be as brutally honest as possible. There will be times you may root for me and there may be times you might say "Woah, he's an asshole." Of course there are moments in our lives we are not proud of such as those times we compromise our morals for our own selfish gain, or don't tell the truth. Some people may decide to suppress them as if they never existed and others may learn from them. For some it may not even phase them.

Whether or not you are on my side, your opinion is right because life is all about your interpretation and reaction to everything around you. I have no say in that. Please enjoy your interpretation of my first year living in Salt Lake City, Utah.

My name is Aaron Jones and I lived in Salt Lake City, Utah. Though, I grew up in Portland, Oregon. I currently reside in Seattle, Washington with some time spent in Phoenix, Arizona, then briefly moved back to Portland before moving to Salt Lake City. That city that did everything but kill me.

Let's be honest, when you think of exciting cities the first thoughts are probably going to lead you to Los Angeles, New york, San Francisco and possibly Miami. As of late, my home city of Portland may or may not be mentioned in that group as well. Prior to moving to Salt Lake City, confusion was often a main theme. A lot of close peers, friends and acquaintances often asked "Why would you move there?" or "you know there's nothing to do there." I always struggled to answer that question and the answer about why I decided to move changed so often, that even to this day I still do not have a straight answer.

I grew up in the suburbs of Portland and fit the bill of someone who would be a lifelong resident. I grew up in a town called Beaverton which lies about 5 miles west of Portland. The City of Beaverton is home to the Nike world campus, Columbia world headquarters and Intel has one of its largest plants in the world one city over.

I had a normal childhood that consisted of hanging out behind local convenience stores with friends, sleepovers filled with junk food, video games and the occasional run in with alcohol and weed, which was an inconsistent occurrence as well. Everything in my life was just fine. It was not until the summer before my senior year of high school that things changed. During the latter half of my Junior year of high school, I met my friend Blair Adams through some mutual friends. Blair was LDS (Church of Jesus Christ of Latter Day Saints.) Blair and I to this day are still friends however at that time we quickly became best friends. Blair lived in close proximity to me and we had a mutual love for the video game "Halo." The hours spent playing Halo and asking numerous questions about the church were endless.

I had no limits on what I would ask. These questions ranged from ghosts, to aliens, and all the way to cults. A lot of those early questions really did not revolve around the central dogma, practices, or even beliefs of the church. Blair would try his best to answer all the questions I threw his way, but some of my questions really did not have an answer other than pure speculation. If my memory serves me right, this would have begun around late April/early May of 2009. As time went on we would meet to play Halo and my questions would progress to deeper and deeper levels of questioning. Blair's parents would eventually get involved.

I consider Blair's parents family. Blair's Father, Tim is a very devout LDS member. He works his blue-collar job of painting houses and loves his family. Tim is a self-educated man when it comes to the scriptures. Specifically, the Old Testament. He is truly one of the best people I know. Blair's Mother, Katie is the quintessential LDS mother. She is caring, sweet and uses the teaching of the LDS church to raise her children. She has done a great job.

Since Tim was very knowledgeable in the scriptures, he would often join us as we played video games when his schedule would allow. He helped answer a lot of my questions. Their closeness as a family is what made me a family member by association. That is the type of family they are.

As time went on I would eventually end up at the Adam's home for dinner and family parties on a nightly basis. The relationship that began with my friend, Blair, was now transforming into a second family.

My family is great, do not get me wrong. Growing up, my siblings and I were not very close. My parents split for nine years starting when I was 14 so my Father was absent for roughly 60 percent of my teenage years. My older brother and I had a strained relationship at the time, we are now on better terms. My older sister left Portland once the opportunity came after high school. She received a basketball scholarship to Clark College in Vancouver, Washington. From there, her and her high school sweetheart moved back to his home in Hawaii. She now lives in Oakland, California without him.

My little sister, Where to begin? If teenage angst hit anyone harder I would love to see it. As much as I love her, she made life too difficult for herself and as hard as she is trying, she still is not fully recovered. Often there were nights she had drunkenly repented to me and swore to change her ways. I, to this day have a letter from her that she gave to me the morning of January 21, 2011. More on that letter later.

Rather than go into detail about my conversion to the LDS church, I will instead, give a Reader's Digest version of July, 2009 to January, 2011. As time went on, the Adam's family would eventually invite me to church. I was reluctant at first but eventually I said yes to a question that would alter the course of my life.

Every so often you can take a look back at your life and pinpoint exact moments when your life changed. For me, I can without a doubt look back at the first time I agreed to go to church and know This was my moment. It was not some huge awakening experience, a loss of a loved one or some grand fortune I came upon. It was simply a church service that would take three hours out of my otherwise uneventful Sunday. Not only did I attend church in mid-May but I would continue to attend church with the Adam's family throughout the rest of the summer and into the fall.

I went so often that I began to meet with the missionaries, Elders Haviland and Harris. I would take the missionary lessons at the Adams home as well. In order to be baptized into the LDS church by a male holding the "proper authority," one must meet with the missionaries. One thing that sticks out from those lessons was how unbelievably boring they were, at times. Thinking back, I can honestly say I am almost positive I fell asleep in one of those lessons. A missionaries goal is to baptize. There are other goals as well, but as a missionary your biggest goal is to grow the local congregations through the waters of baptism. I was the missionaries goal.

"Will you Follow the example of Jesus Christ and be baptized by someone holding the proper priesthood authority of God?" was the question Elder Haviland asked me one day in early June. Back at that time I felt a conversion that changed my doubts to beliefs. I believed I truly felt a conversion. I believed and trusted the new morals, creed and doctrine. I agreed I would be baptized and the date would be set for July 18, 2009.

July 18th, 2009 came and I entered the waters of baptism. I was now a member of the Church of Jesus Christ of Latter-Day Saints. The local congregations of the church consists of Wards. Similar to a Catholic Parish, a group of Wards is called a stake. A stake is similar to a Catholic Diocese.

I was a member of the Oak Hills Ward of the Cedar Mill Stake. I attended services faithfully every Sunday. I went to a weekly get together called Mutual at the church with the other youth. I prayed, I read my scriptures and I even gave talks during the main part of the service called Sacrament. As what may or may not be expected though, I went against church doctrine and teachings when it came to certain habits.

I truly believed in the essential aspects of the Church of Jesus Christ of Latter-Day saints. I believed that Joseph Smith was a prophet that restored the church of God. To me, the Book of Mormon was the word of God. I believed God ruled his church through modern-day revelation that only, then President and Prophet, Thomas S. Monson was able to receive. You name it, I believed it. Even if it sounded outrageous, I gave it the benefit of the doubt.

I did not act on it though. I routinely drank Friday nights and was just like any normal high school teenager, except for Sundays. Come Sunday I would "repent" speak of my blessings, pray for others and act like the golden convert. I lived as though I knew if I followed the Church's teachings my life would be full filled. I think back on that time and think if I was drinking and smoking why would I waste my time? I still don't have an answer, however, I do not regret it.

From the early days of my conversion I was often asked about whether I was willing to serve a mission. My answers were generally "Oh, I'm not sure yet." Or "I'll decide later, Right now I'm still figuring things out." I always had the idea of a two year mission in the back of my mind. As time went on, my curiosity of serving a mission turned to a desire.

When it came to serving a mission I had two main reasons for wanting to serve. The proper answer, according to what those in the church would often hear me say was "I want people to enjoy the blessings I've had from converting to the Church." The other reason(which was my main motivation) was that the thought of moving was exhilarating to me. I do not come from a wealthy family and I had awful grades in high school so that was not going to happen through University. After high school I lacked the openness that I had when it came to moving to Salt Lake City. I would often have imaginative fantasies about going to Paris, London and Italy. As time went on, I decided to prepare for a full-time mission. Things became real for me, whether I was prepared for my mission, or not that was not something I considered.

Even while preparing for my mission I still drank and smoked weed. After high school three of my closest friends went to the University of Oregon. I was alone in my little town of Beaverton. Well, not exactly. My friend to Whom this very book is dedicated to was there with me; Branton Bradford. Branton and I would find any way possible to get down to the city of Eugene, Oregon.

Neither of us had a car so we had to get creative. That often meant checking craigslist for a ride share. When we finally made it to Eugene, we would be so excited to see our friends we forgot all about the pains of getting down there. Those memories are a little fuzzy though because of the copious amounts of alcohol we had drank. I do not think I'll ever drink as much as I did on those early trips to Eugene, both before and after my mission. I love my friends to death and they must love me because they always took care of Branton and I with every visit we made.

Back to the story. In October, 2010 I received my mission call. I stood there in my ex-girlfriend's (she was also LDS) house. Her and I dated for the entirety of my senior year of high school. Her family had put on a brunch for me and members of the ward that were interested in where I would be serving my mission to.

"Elder Jones, you are hereby called to labour in the Arizona

Phoenix Mission." What the fuck? I was expecting to have been sent off somewhere way more exciting than Phoenix, Arizona! I would later learn everything in Arizona wants to kill you. The scorpions, the sun, the drivers and just the desert as a whole. Nevertheless, I still planned on serving and I did so from January 2011 to January 2013.

I will always remember the morning I left. I went into my little sisters room and she handed me a letter while she was still laying in her bed. I did not have time to read the letter until I was in the terminal waiting to board my plane. As I read the letter, I got to see a side of my sister that I had never seen before. She was open with her love for me as a brother. She mentioned things that came to mind later on while living in Salt Lake City. It was a tender moment for me, since that letter was written and read my sister and I have become great friends. It is something that should I be stripped of everything I own and begging for change on the streets of Seattle, I won't ever give up or loose.

I won't spend a lot of time speaking of my mission because no book can contain the love I have for the time I served as a missionary.

While I am no longer a member of the Church of Jesus Christ of Latter-day Saints, I look back at my mission with love. As a missionary, your purpose is to preach the gospel of Jesus Christ. The gospel is the core doctrine of the church.

If it was not for my mission I would not be the person I am today.

After my mission, I returned to Portland for roughly eighteen months. A month after my mission, I had a night of weakness and gave into alcohol and marijuana.

I grew up in a neighborhood full of other neighborhood kids my age. We routinely spent every summer exploring the small lake at the end of the apartment complex, running around the creek and walking under the bridge. It was the best childhood I could have ever asked for.

One night I arrived at my friend's house and he instantly broke out a joint. He asked me if I wanted to smoke, I obliged, thinking I could just repent the next day.

We decided to go to dinner and we were both pretty high. The server asked me something that I had yet to be asked since I had turned 21. "Would you like a drink menu?" I agreed. Her next question was "What would you like to drink?" Without hesitation, I said "Guinness." I drank two with my dinner that night.

This was odd for several reasons, for one, this was only a month after my mission and I really do not like dark beer. Even now, I gravitate more toward sours, ciders and the cheap stuff. Those two beers got me really drunk. The next day, being slightly hungover, I felt guilty and repented.

From there, it was a downward spiral. I learned a lot about myself during this period. I had tasted the happiness and excitement of leaving home through my mission and now that I was home I hated it. I loved my friends and family but to be home when I could be elsewhere drove me crazy. I wanted to create my own memories with people I had never met before while walking down streets I had yet to traverse and live a life free from my home, family and friends. I wanted to bust my ass for something and not have anyone intercede and take that away from me. Moving to a new city would give me the opportunity to create myself anew. My older sister set the example of leaving right after high school and I would always hear her stories retold through my mother. I was jealous. I wanted those memories for myself.

Call it what you will, but I wanted more from my life. I wanted to be able to say something to the effect of "yeah, I lived there for awhile." Or "Yeah, I lived in Salt Lake City when (insert big world changing event) happened." Moving to a new city and starting over sounded fascinating, and I'm sure for some people it was, is, and will be for future generations. However, in my case, I knew a couple of people from my experience with the Church of Jesus Christ of Latter Day Saints. So it was not a 100% fresh start. Later on though, in my experience, it came as close as it can get.

Salt Lake City is truly a beautiful place. From the Salt Lake Temple to the Wasatch Front in the winter time, it is one of the best kept secrets in the country.

My previous statement is more an opinion, though. Because of the culture and the overbearing presence of the church, there tends to be a black cloud placed over the city, as well as, the State of Utah. The stranglehold the Church has on the state of Utah is often referred to by locals and other people familiar with the church as the "Zion Curtain."

However, There is a counterculture that is well represented. There is SLUG magazine (Salt Lake UnderGround) which concentrates mostly on the local arts, music and alternative lifestyles of Salt Lake City. There is the radio station KRCL, which concentrates a lot on local arts and musical artists. The movie "SLC PUNK" centers on the punk scene that was very strong in the late 80's and early 90s in the Salt Lake valley.

Moving to a new city is anything but easy. Millennials (me being one) have such an idea that has and continues to be painted through various platforms of what it'll be like, but as much as media outlets such as Buzzfeed continually try to paint the picture of what It's actually like, It's just not true. I was one of those who felt the excitement of reading such articles only to find out it was a lie. Do I regret the move? Hell no. Would I go back in time and relive my first year? Hell no.

I decided September 29th 2014 would be my day of departure. September 28th was the day of the first PBR music festival in Portland. PBR fest is a music festival put on by Pabst Blue Ribbon. My friends and I watched Modest Mouse play a two-hour set, grabbed a burrito from Chipotle and the next day I began my drive to Salt Lake City.

SLC or Bust
Chapter 1

The morning came and it was time for me to leave. I had arrived home the night before around midnight and woke up around 4:00 am. Needless to say, I was sleep deprived and even had second thoughts about waiting another day. I pushed those thoughts away and continued with my plan. My childhood dog, Ethel or as I refer to her, "felipe" cries when she sees luggage so I had all my baggage and belongings that I needed to start a new life in the garage. I did not want to hear her lonesome cry.

Leaving home, I knew it was going to be difficult but I can always text or call my family. Felipe was a different story though. She was easily my best friend. I didn't want her to see the luggage and know I was leaving her. I pulled my little Toyota corolla around the back and loaded everything in that would fit. I packed my life up in 3 suitcases a record player and a sleeping bag. Blankets and pillows were scattered about.

I began to shake and if I was to speak I would have been reduced to tears. The reason I shook this way was because it was at this point that all the planning, all the telling of friends and acquaintances I was moving to Salt Lake City, was finally here. After I had finished loading my car, I went to say goodbye to my family. It was just my Mother and I home at this point. My mom hastily gave me a hug then went back to bed. I saw Felipe sleeping toward the end of the

bed like she usually does. I gave her a belly rub, and a kiss on the snout and that was all I could bear to do. Felipe is my childhood dog and nothing can prepare you to leave your childhood dog who coincidentally, is also your best friend. I also said goodbye to my other dog Lucy(RIP). She was old, fat and grumpy so that wasn't nearly as hard. I walked downstairs to my car, put it in drive, and I was gone.
The drive itself was not very notable. I drove through eastern Oregon bored out of mind, only to have thoughts of suicide as I drove through Idaho. If you ever get the chance to visit Idaho, don't. It's not worth it.
I will say however, there were two highlights in Idaho. The first being the town of Idaho Falls. In Idaho Falls there is a massive canyon that is in the middle of endless fields and crops. It literally comes out of nowhere. The canyon is massive and gorgeous.

The other, is when you cross into northern Utah. Not that northern Utah is anymore exciting or spectacular, but you can be rest assured that you are not in Idaho anymore.

My destination in Utah was a town called Tooele. Tooele is a small town that lies on the southern end of the Great Salt Lake. Salt Lake City is about 35-45 minutes northeast of Tooele.

Tooele is such a small city that it took 100 years since the town's founding to reach 30,000 in terms of population. The town was originally meant to hold cattle for the winter because there was plenty of grass and feeding areas that stretched for miles, uninterrupted.

If I were to come up with a metaphor for Tooele it would be "You come because you have to, you stay because you don't have a choice".

The reason I came to this town was for my friend, Matt Trussell. Matt was one of my many companion's on my mission. Him and I quickly became great friends. A lot of this had to do with having to spend so much time together. We did not have much in common, but when on the mission and you have the chance to speak of culture and the real world comfortably in such a diluted surrounding, you take it. Before I moved, I had mentioned to him I was planning on moving to Salt Lake City. He graciously offered to let me stay with him rent free until I found work and a place to live.

His offering to do so is what really motivated me to move because it took out a lot of worry and stress that would inevitably happen. Through all my excitement, nervousness and anxiousness, I never looked up where Tooele actually was.

I arrived at Matt's apartment only to find him not home. I had about a thirty minute wait for him to arrive. I didn't want to sit in my car so I decided I would grab my penny board and skate around the neighborhood that was now my home. As I penny-boarded around I couldn't help

but smile to myself. I was finally beginning a new life.
As I looked around and saw the West side of the Oquirrh mountains for the first time, I took a breath of the fresh Utah air and I finally felt the feeling of independence that I had hoped to feel.
A short time later, Matt arrived and after a brief reunion I would drive another hour to Provo to see one of my favorite local Portland artists, Matt Dorrien. I drove like a maniac down the back country roads that would lead me to a city called Provo. The concert was at the old Muse Cafe, which was at that time located in the heart of downtown Provo. The Muse Cafe has since relocated to another part of downtown.
After breaking speeding laws, running stop signs and struggling to find parking, I arrived at the venue. I walked in eager and excited to get a glimpse of one of my favorite aspects of home; the local music scene. I arrived to see that the artist I had come

to see was not playing. I believe I was one of 10 other people there so I walked up to him and asked "have you played yet?" He replied "I finished about five minutes ago." I was bummed. Thinking back on that moment, it is a good metaphor for how my first year in Salt Lake City would go. Which, in a broader sense, is nothing would go the way I hoped it would.

That night rather than drive back to Tooele, I stayed in Provo with some friends from Portland. They are what you call "good ole Mormon boys." That night consisted of catching up, IHOP and video games. It is important to note that at this time I really wanted to give the Church another chance. Ever since I was a member I always had the intent to have been an active member of the Church but as Christians love to say, "satan" is behind your wrong choices.

My idol Hunter S. Thompson put it simply "No sympathy for the devil… and if it Occasionally gets a little heavier than what you had in mind, well… Maybe chalk it off to forced conscious expansion: Tune in, freak out, get beaten." This was a philosophy that as I began to take on, would coincide with the demise of my accountability to the teaching of the LDS church and christianity as a whole for that matter.

I would be in Provo again in a matter of days.

When I returned from my mission, I was still in contact with my mission President. One tradition among returned mission presidents is holding a mission reunion. My mission president was no exception. As time would go on, while living in Salt Lake City, I would speak to my mission President, Sporadically at best. One of the reason I had moved to Utah was to be closer to my fellow return missionaries. I had imagined being close with them and assumed every Friday, Saturday and Sunday we would be together. They would be there to help edify me, support me and

help me do the right thing in relation to the gospel.
This was not my reality.
I drove to Provo excited and anxious to see those I had served with. This was to be the culmination of my move and was suppose to confirm one of the very reasons I had packed up and moved my entire life.
I got there ahead of Matt and others that I was also very close mission friends with. I had been home for almost two years at this point. There were a lot of fellow returned missionaries I did not know and had never met. Too many unfamiliar faces for me to truly feel comfortable. I awaited the arrival of those that were among my favorites.
They eventually arrived and we caught up like the old friends we were. I spoke about my recent move to Salt Lake City, my career aspirations and plans to get married in the temple just like everyone else.
I had a great time seeing the people I loved. It was that night that I realized something. As

much as I loved seeing those from my mission, they had gone back to their own lives. While I had nothing against that, that is when I learned that my move would not be as seamless of a transition as I thought. I tried to ignore those thoughts because facing the reality would begin to uproot my belief system because the support I yearned for was not going to be a reality.

Of course there was nothing wrong with them going back to their own lives, I just didn't take that into consideration upon my move. I assumed everyone would feel that same sense of camaraderie I felt and would push for the same thing.

Provo is where my mission reunion was and Provo is a different type of beast all by itself. It is home to BYU and the city just north of it, Orem, is home to Utah Valley University. Both cities are in incorporated Utah county.

Utah county holds the distinction of being the highest LDS population per county in the world. Along with the church, Utah is also notorious for its fraud. It's the worst kind of fraud as well, it's legal fraud. Pyramids schemes are legal due to the passing SB 182 in 2006. This bill was lobbied by companies such as Nu skin being present at all hearings.

Utah county itself is responsible for nearly half the fraud cases in Utah. Most, if not all, companies that practice such schemes aren't breaking the law while in Utah. They are technically law-abiding companies with law-abiding citizens. However, if they held themselves accountable to the church standards (which presumably they hold themselves to) when asked the question "Are you honest in your dealings with your fellow man?" the hope would be that many hold themselves truly accountable to the higher law they prescribe to and not the temporal law they are ethically breaking. Of course, assuming is never good. However, I will make an educated guess that the majority of them

are LDS. According to the 2010
census, 81.2 percent of Utah
county residents are LDS. That
breaks down to at least four out
of every five residents residing
in Utah county lines being LDS.
Utah does not have state lottery.
No scratch-it's, no state
powerball and no gambling at all.
Utah has found a way to still
make revenue and that is through
the legalization of pyramid
schemes and allowing those
companies to flourish.
The next day I had a job
interview that was previously
scheduled while in Oregon. More
on this later. After the
interview, the moment I had
waited for was finally here. I
was going to have the rest of the
day to explore my new city. I
wasn't really ready for the
underwhelming size of Salt Lake
City. The size of central
downtown encompasses about 6
square blocks of downtown proper.
As time passed, I came to
appreciate it more and more. But
at first I was definitely very
disappointed.

That day, I walked by restaurants that I would share memories in, bars I would spend time in with friends trying to work up enough courage to talk to the cute girl across the room and even the street corners I would cry on. The first time exploring my new city was a beautiful feeling and a moment that gave me mixed emotions. I missed Portland but I was eager to begin a new life where no one knew who I was and I wasn't defined by my past. I was excited to meet new people and have new experiences. Little did I know at that time, they would be months down the road.

I headed back out to Tooele after a couple of hours spent exploring. As much as I was happy to have a place to stay, Tooele wasn't anywhere near where I wanted to be. I would spend hours on end looking for a place to live downtown. I didn't have any success at all. I would call 10 people a day and I was lucky to hear back from even one. Until I met with Sylvia.

Sylvia was my first Landlord in Salt Lake, and quite possibly the cutest little old woman around town. After a week in Tooele, I moved into a basement apartment in Salt lake City. I moved to neighborhood called the Avenues. The avenues were the first neighborhood in Salt Lake City to deviate from the traditional grid system, which is the reason the vast majority of roads in Salt Lake City run from North to South, East to West.
The Avenues have been the home to everyone from a once infant, later to-be, church president, to a serial killer named Ted Bundy. A large portion of the Avenues is occupied by the Salt Lake Cemetery. The Salt Lake Cemetery is the oldest and the most hauntingly mesmerizing cemetery in the city.
I was in love with my new neighborhood. The Avenues truly are beautiful.
The apartment was and still is located at 1st avenue and C street. The location of the apartment is within walking

distance of central downtown, which is exactly one of the reasons I took the apartment. There was another reason though. I had come to the conclusion (again) that I was going to strive to be a strong and active LDS member. Along with being close to downtown, it was also about four blocks away from Temple Square.

Temple square is the headquarters of the church. This is the location of the Salt Lake City temple, church headquarters, the conference center and a number of church museums.

I would often have visions of what it would be like to have the perfect LDS family that would take walks down to Temple Square while counting our blessings and sing hymns along the way. The same thought now does not appeal to me, whatsoever.

During my time at 1st and C street, I was unemployed. I had been waiting to hear back from my interview earlier but it ended up being a three-week hiring process. Though at that time I did not know it would end up being three weeks. I would often have anxiety about not getting the job and having to move back to Portland with my tail between my legs and humbled beyond belief. I moved to Utah with $700 and that was quickly dwindling. It was during this time that I became ill and couldn't talk at all. It was really strange. I felt fine in every aspect but my throat was swollen shut for the better half of three weeks. I couldn't eat a solid meal and was reduced to tipping my neck slightly to the right to drink water. I lost roughly 10 pounds during this time.

This is where Sylvia comes in. Sylvia was sweet and took pity on me. She was constantly on my case about work, friends and when I became sick, drinking her well-intentioned, but tasteless homemade tea. As sweet as she was and accommodating as she was, this wasn't going as I had planned. As time progressed and my money dwindled I was reduced to watching Netflix in the basement apartment that I had come to hate due to four very distinct reasons.

The first was the lack of natural light. I really didn't think this factor through at all. I never realized how much I really depended on this. Even now I need my blinds up and if I'm inside too long, cabin fever sets in and I need some good tunes and a walk around whatever neighborhood I'm residing in to reset myself. The second being, I was beginning to associate it with being sick. My mood wasn't the best since all I wanted to do was explore, but my reality was driving 650 miles to be in an apartment with very little natural light and watching Netflix which is exactly what I was doing a couple of weeks earlier in Beaverton. The third was my sickness. I have never been more miserable in my life than when I was that sick. More on my sickness later.

The fourth and the biggest reason were the bugs. I saw everything from ants, to cockroaches to house centipedes and yes, even

spiders. Anyone who knows me knows I hate bugs. As much as I loved Sylvia,
her lack of sympathy surprised me. Her response was "oh, they won't hurt you." I don't give a fuck if they won't hurt me, it's even being in the same room and knowing they're around.
Bugs aside, my sickness lingered and lingered. One day I was sick of being in a basement apartment with no natural night and stagnant air. I decided I would find a park in the city, lie down on a blanket and listen to my all time favorite band, Portugal The Man. Mind you, I've been sick for about two weeks at this time so I was wearing a hoodie, athletic shorts and my oldest pair of vans. I finally arrived at Sugarhouse park. Random Fact; Sugarhouse Park is where one of the first activists to speak out about and push for workers rights, was executed. Joe Hill. Sugarhouse park is the location of the old jail house in Salt Lake City.

I quickly found a spot under some trees facing the mountains. I had never been so close to mountains in such a casual setting. The feeling of being so close to the canyons and mountains was very overwhelming but gave me a peaceful feeling. As time went on, I threw the other end of the blanket over me because I was beginning to feel cold. It was an unusually warm October day. However, since I was sick, it didn't feel the way it actually was. I passed out for about three hours. I woke up to my phone dead, pitch blackness and I'm sure people were assuming I was homeless. With my back hurting and my blanket needing to be washed, I headed home.
The next morning I woke up to my throat still bothering me. At this point, I did not have health insurance but I couldn't do it anymore. It had been two weeks of a lingering sickness. I decided to go the hospital that morning. When I arrived at the hospital they asked a question I never realized was so humbling and

embarrassing if not answered right. They asked "do you have insurance?" In my impoverished, weak and frail voice I struggled and replied with a simple "no." I felt myself shrink and immediately regret my decision. On a sheer personal level I could have backed out but I felt I really needed to be checked out. After about twenty minutes of waiting, I was called into the emergency room. During the half hour visit they tested me for strep and mono. Both of which came back negative and that was it. I was sent on my way still in pain and no solution presented. I was humbled and embarrassed by this trip. I was even more humbled when I received the bill. My total owed was over $700. The fact that I didn't have health insurance and was tested for strep and mono does not justify $700 by anyone's standard. Nor should it be normalized. This is the reality for many Americans. People are having to choose between proper health or a life full of debt.

I'm thankful for the fact that it was only $700 and it wasn't an appendix or anything more serious. My parents at the time were not working so I was not able to be on my parents insurance. In previous conversations with people whom are opposed to the Affordable Care Act (Obamacare) they seem to think it's a no brainer that I would be insured because of my parents. In a perfect world, this is a viable option. However those that are opposed, need to realize it's not always an option nor is it always a reality. I cannot imagine the stress that must put on parents to know that if they are not working they are leaving their child's health vulnerable. What the fuck kind of system is that? The american healthcare system is broken and the ACA is the best solution we've had, Though, not perfect, the philosophy behind it is what will save many and will continue to save millions of Americans if done correctly.

As time went on, I would eventually recover and begin to fall in love with Utah. I still had a big problem though, the bugs. Time after time, I would talk to Sylvia and the conversations were to no avail. I'm convinced she was the oldest hippie living in the Salt Lake Valley. She did not like me killing the bugs because she wanted them to live. There are exponentially millions of bugs per human. The respective different species will be ok if I kill a couple.

She gave me this naturopathic powder that was supposed to keep the bugs away but the bugs did not give two shits about the powder. Seriously, the bugs didn't even think twice about this powder.

The deal breaker happened one day when I was taking a shower. I turned around to see a spider about the size of quarter. I was screaming internally! I had to control my breathing and quickly but calmly get the hell out of the shower. I told Sylvia that day I would be moving within the week.

I knew I would have to swallow my pride and give Matt a call. Matt did not hesitate to say yes. I was truly thankful for this. After three weeks, I would be heading back to Tooele under the same stipulation as before; Rent free. This would not always be the case. Tooele would prove to be a very pivotal moment in my life in the fact that my decision to be a member of the church would go from 70/30. The higher of the two being my desire to be an active member of the church to 30/70. The higher of the two representing a growing disaffiliation. This was of course only confined within me and no one else. I was too insecure and unsure about myself at this point in my life to make a decision based on my true happiness. I cared too much about the opinions of others. I did not want to let people down. I wanted the best of both worlds. I wanted to let people know I was an active member of the church, but

I wanted to drink, smoke weed and make mistakes without the dreading fear of repentance. My natural vices and personality wouldn't allow me to be truly active in the church.
I was struggling with the thought that my personality and the person I am was not meant or shaped for the gospel. How can this be though? The gospel and the church teachings are meant for everyone. I can't be an exception, can I? This mentality and the beginning of this acceptance was fought hard at this point. I was a sheepish 22-year-old that had not grown into my own mentality of the person I was going to be. I was not capable of making this type of change. Life in one year would force me to grow mentally in ways I could not have ever imagined.

Three months too long
Chapter 2

I drove back out to Tooele with the thought of "dammit." I wasn't exactly in a state of mind that left me thankful. Instead, it left me bitter in the fact that this wasn't as easy as I had been hoping. I didn't expect it to be easy, but I had the thought that being a member of the church in Utah would make things easier. Eventually I would come to chalk that one up to being young and naive. Why was this happening to me? This would later turn into the broader question that is as old as religion itself, which would torment me for months on end. Why do bad things happen to good people? This question alone can best be answered in the fact that if there is a god, he clearly does not care to deal with our humanly and temporal affairs. The church's answer to this question is "free agency," which is the ability to choose for yourself. This means essentially that God will not interfere with someone's actions even if someone who is a god-fearing man is a victim of whatever another person's actions may be, will not be spared. In the LDS church you are taught this came about as a gift from the heavenly father. The ability for us to act for ourselves is a gift from an ominous being somewhere in the universe.

This coincides with the thought that god is a loving heavenly father. I have a hard time believing that god is a loving heavenly father and truly wants what is best for us when kids are starving, parents dying, mass shooting are common-place and terrorist groups can dissolve borders comparable to biblical times.

While I was living in Tooele, Matt and I were still great friends. However, the awkwardness of me settling into his place was becoming evident more and more everyday. I tried my best to be a guest that did little to affect the daily life of Matt. After all, I knew I was a guest because Matt would remind me through various passive aggressive comments.

Tooele was a very lonely time for me. Making friends in the social scene I wanted to be a part of was not going to happen because it did not exist anywhere but Salt Lake City. In this aspect Matt was awesome, he would invite me to nearly everything. I can still remember one of the first texts he sent me "Hey, my families making dinner and watching a movie this sunday and I won't take no for an answer!" This was very flattering and humbling to me because I'm not used to people accommodating me. The dynamic with my closest friends back in Portland isn't even that inviting at times.

Matt's family is awesome. They accepted me as one of their own. As you can probably see this is a pattern when it comes to LDS families. Family importance is drilled into your head at a young age. It truly is a redeeming quality within the church. Just about every Sunday I would join the Trussell family for dinner.

Quoting the english author Paul Auster in regards to friendship: "We crave friendships because we are social beings, born from other beings and destined to live among other beings until the day we die." The Trussell family unknowingly helped quench my thirst for social interaction and friendship in a way that even I didn't know was what I wanted and needed. It wasn't until I reflected on this several months later that I was thankful for their hospitality on Sundays because most weeks that was what I ended up looking forward to most.

As time would go on I would meet some of his friends and although they were all LDS members, they were still going to bars fairly often, but they would not participate in drinking and promiscuity. The bar that was frequented was called the Westerner. The Westerner is a country dancing themed bar in West Jordan, Utah. It is a chance for suburban people to interact with "country folk," which I would later learn from other friends never went very well and often led to fights between the "liberal city people and the conservative country hicks." I never considered myself a country dancer. There was a time in the seventh

grade where we learned how to line dance but even then I had two left feet that seemed to follow me to my adulthood.
I can distinctly remember thinking "what the hell am I doing here?" I danced with girls I never talked to again, burned my hand on a mechanical bull that I'll never ride again and played wingman for guys I'll never talk to again. This had all been done while being sober. This was something I would try to hold onto.
One visit to the Westerner in particular stands out to me because it was the one time in my life I attempted to approach a girl at random. I knew more than ever that this was my chance to prove to myself that moving here was the right move for me. Matt and I were sitting down at the tables at the back right of the main dancing floor. I had noticed this girl from afar and I knew that I had to find a way to talk to her. It would be awkward and awful to watch, but this is why I was here for.

As the night went on and I tried to gather the strength to make my move, I couldn't help but notice how good of a dancer she was and this of course only made it more difficult to talk to her. I wanted to be one of those guys that can easily sweep the girl off her feet by dancing effortlessly and perfectly, but I knew this wasn't going to be the case.

I decided I was going to go over and talk to her anyway. After about 20 minutes of taking myself in and out of it I finally decided to put my plan into action. The plan was to ask her to dance and once I swept her off her feet I would easily get her number. Easy right?

The whole night she had been almost exactly opposite of where we were. If this was going to happen I would have to work for it. All I had to do was be cool, calm and collected.

I began walking towards her and to this day I'm positive she knew I had planned to make my move. Throughout the night, we had made awkward-at-best eye contact several times which made it harder because now she was expecting me to walk over. As I started to approach where she was I froze mid walk and changed my mind. I blew it. I walked to the siding wall that stretched the length of the dance floor and stood there. I stood there very awkwardly for about 10 minutes before I looked over at her, we made eye-contact once again.

After we made eye-contact she began walking towards me. I was internally having a panic attack. She is now the one making the move. I didn't know what she was going to say or do and I could feel myself getting more anxious with every step.

She asked me to dance and boy did that come to a surprise for me. As shocked and as frozen as I was, I knew I had to follow her lead. I was excited and flattered that she had asked me until I remembered that I couldn't dance, my anxiety would come and go as it pleased throughout that first dance. I awkwardly danced with her until the end of the song. At the end of the song I asked her for her number. We exchanged numbers and that was pretty much it. We texted for a bit but nothing stuck and we both went back to our lives. It wasn't anything too climactic but it was enough to leave an impression on me. From that moment I knew I could do this. I made the right decision in starting my new life.

Unbenounced to anyone, were my internal struggles. The church's grasp on me was slipping away more and more everyday through my own negligence. I didn't want Matt to know I was drinking because if he did, I feared I would end up with nowhere to go. This very fear didn't affect my decisions but what it did was make me question myself more. Am I being deceitful to myself or to the church? I wasn't proud to be lying to my friend, but at that time I felt it easier to lie to my friend than to be honest to myself.

While living in Tooele, I worked in a city called South Jordan as a Porter at an apartment complex. Not very glamorous, but I was used to doing these types of jobs. The job of a porter is basically a janitor/groundskeeper which meant usually doing something like picking up trash, laying salt when it's icy or whatever else the manager may ask of you.

The drive from Tooele to South Jordan is easily 45-50 minutes with no traffic. With traffic, I wouldn't be home until seven when I was off at five. I didn't mind it though I've always loved long drives because they give me time to think. It gave me time to really think about the things I didn't even want to remember, the things that I would someday have to face but still kept pushed away. During these drives I had come to the conclusion that my guilt could be ridden in one of two ways: Be active in the church and go through the repentance process or option two, Forsake my beliefs so I would not have to hold myself accountable to them. I was caught in the middle and didn't see an end in sight. When it comes to the church there is no such thing as "middle ground." You're either all-in or all-out. At this point I was playing both.

As mentioned before, I was glad to be working and it could not have come at a better time because Matt had begun to charge me rent. The aforementioned deal was "Rent free" and even though I had a problem with this, it was in his right to do so. I wanted so bad to move out of Tooele and him charging me rent was not going to help. I don't know why he did it. I didn't question it though because I did not want to create tension. As much as I loved Matt, there were times I would often keep my mouth shut because he had a temper that was very passive but noticeable. I paid my rent, no questions asked.

My days off from work were spent in Salt Lake City, mostly at coffee shops. Thinking back on it, I really wish I would have been more proactive when it came to exploring Salt Lake City. Matt didn't have wifi so I would often go to a coffee shop called Sugarhouse coffee. I would order a hot chocolate or a coffee. It all depended on whether I wanted to be LDS that day or not. Yes, I went back and forth that often. While there, I would literally watch Netflix for hours on end, then go to Chipotle just down the street. I really was not making the most out of those days off. However, those days were more exciting than any day spent in Tooele.

I began to spend a lot of time with my friend Lydia. Lydia and I had met online and met when her and her family were visiting Portland. The first time we met up while in Utah was on Halloween. That night I had driven home from work and was back in Tooele, Lydia invited me to a house party later that night. I jumped on the invite and drove to Salt Lake in about twenty minutes. Lydia and I went on to go to several parties that night.

Being on the fringe of the LDS church is interesting when you meet others who are in a similar position. It's a line that you both tip-toe. Neither wants to seem to be a "sinner" because if you're trying to be with them in a romantic sense, you don't want to reveal too much that will lead them to believe you're going to leave the church.

When you're on the fence, it can easily go both ways. If both of you leave the church then it works out great. If both of you want to be active then you have someone there with you. It's a game of not giving into your vices. Not because you want to be a good member of the church, but because you don't know the other person's boundaries or how far they are willing to go.

If you reveal too much and it doesn't work out, then no harm. If you reveal too much and it turns in your favor, then that is the moment things change for either better or worse.

Overall, the night consisted of awkward flirting and catching up. I didn't drink that night, even though I wanted to. In short, Lydia was a pretty fucking awesome girl. I was just an idiot and blew it with her.

The next time we got together was the night of the Oregon vs. Utah game on November 8th, 2014. The night of the Halloween party, one of Lydia's friends had mentioned she had an extra ticket and asked me if I wanted to go. I said "of course," but I didn't want to pursue it because I didn't know her friend very well and I didn't want to appear desperate for the ticket. I ended up securing the ticket and plans were set in stone.

I drove home from work, quickly changed, then turned right around to get to Lydia's house. Her house is literally right next door to Rice-eccles stadium. After some tailgating that was put on by a local radio station, which was as trashy as you can imagine, we ended up back at Lydia's house.

We continued to drink at her house, which surprised me. Again, Lydia was technically LDS like I was but I had never seen her drink. as much as she was on this night. At one point in the night we ended up in her room, just us two. I can easily say I was moderately buzzed at this point and so was she. We had our first intimate moment there in her room. We both were standing very close to each other. Basically side to side. We looked at each other and shared an intimate kiss. We had kissed when we were in Portland, but this was different because the hope of a

relationship was now a reality. It wasn't something that was in the distant future, miles apart was not an issue anymore. This was the moment that those hopes should have come true.
As we sat in her living room with her friends, we continued to drink and slip into a further inebriated state of being. Eventually it was time to go to the game. The game itself is remembered best because a Utah player dropped the ball at the one yard line after an interception. Utah got blown out in the fourth quarter. I hate U of O. for the most part, they are nothing but California bro's and basic girls who get a business degree and take a job at Nike world campus and collectively continue to gentrify the city of Portland. After the game we headed back to Lydia's house. I stayed the night with her.
The next morning as I collected my clothes and awkwardly said goodbye, which consisted of a goodbye kiss and walk to my car, I had a very quiet drive with myself back to Tooele. I felt guilty, and shameful for having sex out-of-wedlock. This would only last about a day though. I felt more guilty and shameful because I was going to have to lie to my friend about the whole night like I had done many times but since living with him, I had never gone this far.

Lydia and I got together a couple more times after that. Lydia is a very funny person and overall she's a catch, but I was just an idiot. I blew it 100 percent. Last I heard about Lydia, she was happily in a relationship and doing well with school. I'm truly happy for her because that's what she deserves. She didn't deserve someone such as myself. We hooked up and the connection on my end wasn't there for whatever reason. She deserved the honesty of that realization, which I never gave her.

At this point you could easily say I was having an identity crisis brought on by self-induced stress. I faced guilt and shame from four different fronts. Each one just as painful, yet distinctly different from the other. Each represented an emotional separation of bonds formed during my many phases throughout my activity in the church. The whirlwind facing me, should the truth come out, was enough to push me to the brink of my emotional limit.

As a missionary you essentially join the closest thing to a fraternity within the church. When I speak to another RM, I can understand some of what they went through. From the hours of door knocking, to the jubilee that a baptism brought and all the way to the sorrow when an investigator didn't fully embrace what you love and even a beloved fellow missionaries service is up and it's their time to go home. There is a sacred bond among RM's because of the truth and conviction both of you shared at one point in your life.

The goal is to stay as close to the "spiritual blessings" you learned on your mission for the rest of your life and by consequence, eternity. When I came home from my mission I wanted nothing more than to be surrounded by my new "brothers." It would be easier to live oblivious to the world as well as the concept of "sin" if I was still as close to the mission as possible.

I would eagerly await other missionaries to return home. I missed The few I was very close with. I wanted to reminisce with them and just for a brief amount of time, feel nostalgic about the two years we spent in Phoenix, Arizona.

For a brief moment in time feel as indestructible as we did riding bike in 115 degree heat, getting drinks thrown at us and laying down at night and wondering if we had busted our asses enough that day for the Lord. I missed those days with all my heart and at certain moments, even now, I find my thoughts are full of my mission and the wonder of what if?

What if I didn't slack on my mission and I could say I worked hard wherever I went? Were there times when I could

have worked harder? Yes. Were there times I broke rules? Yes. Were there times I regretted the mission? No. I had moderate success on my mission and would constantly defend the church against anyone who would try to "Bible bash" with us. Not to toot my own horn, but by the end of my mission, I was very knowledgeable in the scriptures, specifically the new testament. On my mission, I loved the chance I got to take on representatives from other churches. Thinking back on it, a missionary will never admit to losing one of those scrimmages because in the end "We're always right." Letting other fellow returned missionaries down, specifically the ones I had laboured with, was not an option.
One story i'm reminded of from my mission actually took place on my birthday. December 1, 2012. I was in the final two months of my mission. My companion at the time, Elder Wade, was still relatively new to the mission field. Not even out six months. Elder Wade and I visited a family called the Slocums. I had been teaching them for over a year at that point. We decided to visit them in between our lessons just to say hello and check up on them. This was not irregular at all for Elder Wade and I.
The Slocums, whether it was the majority of Cathy's doing, or Rods, had all sorts of old western knickknacks

over all their walls and any other surface, such as coffee tables, night stands and even the entertainment center. The Slocums were from Michigan. I never quite understood their love and obsession for old western knicknacks. One wall had an old metal wheel that would have been used for an old wagon wheel. The other wall had a fur of some sort of animal that met an untimely death. Their home felt like my home, since I was over there so often. I taught the Slocums for so long because they had moved to a new area of the city and I had moved been transferred to that new area.

As they opened the door for us, there was a very somber feeling felt as we walked to the living room. Cathy was not acting herself and talking our ears off, like usual. Rod wasn't filling us in on the daily happenings in the world. They weren't bickering or even fighting, which they had done in front of us a number of times. It was a very eerie feeling from what we had come to know and love from the Slocums.

Rod hastily exited out to the garage and after a few awkward attempts of us trying to keep the conversation going, Cathy asked us to meet Rod in the garage because he had something he wanted to say to us. We quickly made our way to the garage not knowing what to expect. Our nervousness began to set in. The somber mood and the fact they weren't acting themselves caused concern within us.

As we entered the garage and began speaking with Rod, he told us Cathy and him had made their decision. They would not be continuing their missionary lessons, nor entering the waters of baptism. I believe I can speak for Elder Wade when I say both our hearts dropped. I loved these two people with all my heart and for them to do that to us? After over a year of teaching them, investing our time, and praying for them, want nothing to do with our message that was supposedly filled with nothing but blessings and bliss? How can that be possible? We walked back to our car defeated and saddened. I was in the passenger seat. I lost it.

I began furiously hitting the dash as hard as I was able to, almost wanting the airbag to deploy. I began yelling every swear word in the book as if somehow my exertion would take me back in time to say the right things that would bring the Slocums unto the Lord Jesus Christ through the waters of baptism. All Elder Wade could do was pat me on my shoulder. As I began to calm down my anger turned to sadness and depression. My hitting turned to sobbing and whimpering.

It was moments like this that involved so much of every emotion I could muster and be so concerned about someone's personal salvation, I couldn't let fellow return missionaries know I was not harboring the same conviction and testimony as I did at moments such as this. This zeal and willingness to be so emotionally invested wouldn't have been possible though, if it was not for the love and support I received from members of the local congregation back home where those convictions began. Members of the church back home shaped me just as much as anything else during those early years in the church. Back home as mentioned in the Introduction, I was viewed as a stalwart member of the church. I would routinely bear my testimony in front of the congregation and would often be reduced to tears by the "spirit."

Looking back on it, the spirit was being overcome by passion and conviction I had for the church. I've had the same feeling while experiencing other things I'm passionate about.

Back in the local congregation, in Beaverton, there was a man by the name of Brother Taylor. Brother Taylor and I would speak to each other at church activities, church meetings and any other time we would cross paths. His daughter was my age so because of this, I would see him fairly often. He is an awesome man. He is one of the most caring and loving people I've ever met. When it came time to get ready to serve my mission, I didn't have any luggage, nor did I have the means to just

whimsically go out and buy what I needed for the mission.
Brother Taylor gave me a call one day and said something to the extent of 'Hey, do you have luggage for your mission?" I knew what he was about to say, but I sheepishly replied "no, but I'll figure something out, so I'm not too worried." he replied, "Well, we want to help you get ready for your mission so we might as well go buy you some luggage!" I lied when I said I wasn't too worried about it. I was. I didn't have any other option for luggage. I humbly agreed to let the Taylor family buy me luggage for my mission. the luggage they bought for me that day is still in use today. I will forever be thankful for what the Taylor family did for me. It's actions like this I, myself, began to feel almost indebted to members of the church such as the Taylors. At times when I questioned the church, I often thought that church members expected me to stay active, almost as a token of their help that had been rendered in the past. As members of the church would help me prepare, this mentality began to weigh on me. My thought was that if I fell away from the church then they would look at me as ungrateful. Which I most certainly was not, however through this whole process instead of teaching myself that this logic was wrong, I taught myself that that would be the

only possible outcome. The humility it took for me to say yes, was hard for me to accept. Whatever the reason may be, depending on the situation, I mistake my own humility for embarrassment. Some people just need help. I was no exception. The kindness and generosity I felt with my local congregation back home wasn't extraordinary in the context of any other ward. The same selflessness I saw in Portland was something I saw countless times in Phoenix.

When serving a mission, members of the church definitely play a huge role in your day-to-day life. You rely on the members to help you find people to teach and even a hot meal at the end of the day. Ward members on your mission look at the missionaries as brave, young men who are willing to put their lives on hold to share the gospel. They are generally admired by the members and often cause teenage girls within the ward to swoon because a return missionary is looked upon as the ultimate catch and generally a standard for marriage within the church.

You spend a lot of time within the homes of members. Missionaries are seen as "god's army." For a church member to see a missionary no longer active in the gospel, a lot of judgement and shame is brought on at the expense of the once proud missionary.

A family that I became very close with was the Nichols family. My companion at the time, Elder Walpole and I taught the gospel to Brother Nichols, and the younger son, Joey. This led them to be baptized.

During the course of my mission, my clothes began to unravel at the seams, kept stains and began to look unkempt. After one of our lessons, Sister Nichols, whose bluntness we had become very accustomed to, looked at me and said "You need new pants, when is your P-day?"

P-day was our preparation day, which is the equivalent of our day off. P-days were every Monday. Though, it really was not a day off because after six pm we were expected to be out doing missionary work. This was the only day buying new clothes would have been acceptable. The following Monday, Sister Nichols took Elder Walpole and I to Kohl's.

Sister Nichols had me pick out what I wanted. This was everything from ties, to shirts, to pants. This put me in an awkward situation since I didn't really want to bask in the help I was receiving because once again, my humility began to turn into embarrassment. I picked out the bare minimum and only took what I needed. Sister Nichols wouldn't stand for that. she made me pick out a tie. Ties are essentially currency on the mission.

The memories of trading ties with other missionaries are too vast to mention a single instance.

The generosity Sister Nichols shared at this point, was the most extreme case she ever did for us, however it wouldn't be her last. She would routinely drop off food and even money. Accepting money on the mission was supposed to be something you did not do. But we were only given a monthly stipend of $115 for food. In a 31 day month, this was equal to $3.70 a day. Over the course of the six months I taught Brother Nichols and her son, she would constantly have us over for dinner, give us food and offer anything she could do to help us. Sister Nichols is the true definition of a saint. Sister Nichols husband was a convert of mine and he, as well as the Nichols family became, and are still very special to me.

The fourth and possibly worse, are your converts. The time invested in a convert is staggering. For example, going back to the Slocums, for fourteen months in total I taught them. I grew to love them like family. I was blunt with them, I was soft at times and I was always affirming to them the truthfulness of the gospel. On the mission I would constantly hear "if you fall away, so will your converts." Well, put that on me why don't you? This is a church's version of an old wives tale. This one is considered dangerous because If the person who taught them the gospel is him/herself doubting the very thing they bore with utter conviction and zeal, doubting the very thing they centered their lives on for two years, then it might shake their convert to their core if their conversion wasn't strong in the first place.

One example; on my mission I met a young man that was almost identical to me. I had just been transferred to Surprise, Arizona from Sedona. I was bummed to have left one of the most beautiful places in the country. Dominic's friend Jake had invited him to church that sunday. This, coincidentally, was my first sunday in that area. My new companion at the time was Matt Trussell. Dominic and I met and we began teaching him. Him and I instantly formed a bond that still lasts to this day. Dominic was baptized by his best friend, like me. Dominic was baptized the only member of his family, like me. Dominic was only two years younger than me and would often fill us in on what was going on in the world. Dominic was and continues to be a great person. Dominic was our pride and joy as missionaries. We loved working with him, as well as his friend, Jake. I looked at him as a younger brother of sorts. As time would go on, I would learn that Dominic

would at times look up to me because of
how similar our paths to the gospel
were. I felt I needed to stay active
for Dominic. I couldn't let dominic
know I was questioning the church's
validity.
I loved my converts with all my heart,
I really did. I couldn't let them down.
It's a similar feel to the scene in
Forrest Gump when he is running in
southern Utah and he simply decided he
is going to go home and not have
anything to do with running anymore.
the decision to stop doing what he
clearly loved and by consequence,
others came to love, was enough to
leave those following him disheveled
and confused. Once he stops, other
people stop because their reason for
joining, was done.
Was this to be the reality of my
situation? Probably not, but I didn't
want to risk it. The thought of this
would keep me up at night tossing and
turning because I couldn't bare being
someone's reason to leave, just as
easily as I was their reason to be
baptized.
As much as I love all these people,
they are exceptions to continued
communication from the mission
regardless of religious beliefs. As
soon as the common denominator is gone,
so too is whatever the status of our
friendship was. It makes you realize
how shallow the friendship was.

As time went on, I began to feel like I was stuck in a square.
All around me were my converts, members in Portland, as well as in phoenix and fellow missionaries, both returned and still serving. In the center was me. Not that their lives revolved around me, but they were always present in mine whether they realized it or not. The four points of guilt I just made represent each side. As long as I'm active in the gospel, it's a perfectly shaped square and were all coexisting within the gospel. If I begin to show signs that I'm leaving or even beginning to question the gospel, the square starts to get smaller and smaller until eventually it has collapsed on itself, which by that definition, collapses on me. The collapse represents the full capacity of their judgements, and condemnations upon me. It represents their lack of letting me be open-minded and use my "free agency" to not be a part of the gospel. One can easily say "Aaron, why do you bother with their opinion? These are people who shouldn't matter when it comes to living your life." This would take the refiner's fire for me to come to that realization.
In the church anyone who leave is looked at for lacking something. I couldn't bare the thought of being looked at as lacking something. It can be a lack of prayer, or scripture

study, because of what you lack, the consequence is your testimony of the church not being as strong as it should be. It could be carelessness, and the willingness to let such a divine gift go. No one who leaves the church is looked at as an equal peer. They are looked down and their name is then mentioned with a negative connotation and implied ruthlessness and rebellious behavior. There is no logical reason for leaving the church in the eyes of the faithful church goer. I had such zeal and faith at one point that I couldn't bare to be thrown into that mix. This was seen to me as embarrassing and that I failed people in those four different groups thus creating the collapse.

All my accomplishments on my mission would go to waste in the eyes of the church. Their opinions would be swift to forget what I did and quick to realize my sins and faults. They would be quick to define me for what I shrunk down to and what I did not grow to be. I would be looked at as someone who couldn't live a righteous life and felt it was easier to live in sin than aspire for something great. The fact that I had a theological change wouldn't come off as justification. Instead, it would be summed up as a lack of education in spiritual matters and an unwillingness to repent and "put away the natural man." The reason for the squares collapse is me not being able to deal with lying anymore and putting on a fake face in a world of fake perfection.

The reason for the collapse is me realizing this isn't what I want anymore and dealing with the loss of so many special people in my life. Then again, I could easily not take their opinion into consideration and walk away with no remorse and not a care in the world. However, I almost felt indebted to them for the love they had shown me. I felt indebted because of the emotion they had brought out of me. I felt indebted because of the bonds we had formed labouring in the Lord's vineyard. I felt indebted because of the material things they bought me that helped me show people eternity. I felt guilty for betraying their trust they once had in me as a messenger for a deity they as well as I, professed to love. This would keep me up at night when I would waver like a ship on the sea looking for land that would help me live the gospel, or staying out at sea and living in a life full of "sin" and using my "free agency" how I wanted to- in a way that wasn't in line with the gospel and by consequence not in harmony with the people in the church I had come to love.

The only people I was very open with were the people I worked with at the apartment complex. I loved working with

them. My direct supervisor was a man named Tim. Tim was a Midwesterner who grew up in South Dakota. Tim drove one of the biggest dodge trucks I've ever seen, wore a camo beanie, and looked like he was born and bred in the backwoods of the south. Tim wanted to end up in either my hometown of Portland, Oregon or Austin, Texas. The reason being how liberal he was. This was a very pleasant surprise. Tim and I bonded over sports and politics.
Rob is an awesome down-to-earth dude who doesn't have a negative word to say about anyone. He is the type of guy who would say "what's up?" Every single time I walked into the office which was often, at least, 10 times a day. Rob is still a close friend of mine to this day. Carlos was a person that I had literally nothing in common with. Him and I had the type of relationship, I would describe as brotherly. Carlos has his shit together. He is in his early twenties and just bought a house. I have all the respect in the world for him. Actually, we do have one thing in common. We both love the song "I will be back one day" By lord Huron. Super random, but he loves that song.
A lady by the name of Heidi was the business manager. Heidi was essentially the mom of the group. We would often have staff lunch courtesy of her and when it came time to decorate the

christmas tree, she made sure we did it as a staff.
As time went on though, I did not love my job, just the people I worked with. I knew being a porter would not be a great or a fulfilling type of job. I was just desperate for a job. Tim's girlfriend, Cricket worked for the same company but at a different property. She was a business manager, as well. The property she worked at was a gorgeous set of downtown buildings that individually, were all over 100 years old. they cumulatively were called the Covey apartments. They resided in the avenues,so they were right in the center of downtown. Cricket had a job opening for a leasing agent and I wanted it desperately for several reasons. The first was I wouldn't be a porter anymore. I wouldn't be working outside and can rest assured I'll be at a desk for the winter. The second was the fact it was central to downtown, the exact place I wanted to be.
In the weeks before I was to leave for christmas vacation I would begin the transferring process. As luck would have it, the renovation of one of the buildings managed by the covey would be something I would help with. The building being renovated was the called the Meredith.
The Meredith was well over 100 years old and looked it. The outside brick was a pale yellow, and had clearly seen

better days. The Meredith clearly had history to it. Before the renovation, the building was a in an awful state of decay. It had been used as government housing for years and the tenants that left, seemed to not care about preserving their home.

I began working on the Meredith before the trash-out had begun. the property management was the company I was with, Alliance. They essentially told them they had to leave in two months or be evicted. People left the place trashed. during the renovation it was not uncommon to find syringes all over the place. Some used, some not.

It was during this time, when working on the renovation, I sat down with Cricket as well as s less than admirable of a person, Spencer the regional manager. I didn't know Spencer was a degenerate human being, but I would eventually learn that later on. During the interview, Cricket was very tough and Spencer was very subservient to Cricket. Which would make sense. Cricket has this very dominating presence. Mostly because she knows exactly what she was talking about and didn't allow anyone to question her. A couple of days after the interview, I was called in to Crickets office and she said "We're gonna take a chance on you." The date of my start was chosen as December 29, 2014. I was sad to be leaving my property in South Jordan, but in the end I needed to do what was best for me. Tim understood that, which was greatly appreciated.

As time got closer for me to go home for christmas, so was my time dwindling in South Jordan. This was obviously sad for me. My co-workers had helped make the transition to Utah a lot easier. though they didn't know it at the time, simply just passing time and talking was generally my only social interaction with someone that day. My start date at the Covey was the day after I was to arrive back in Utah from christmas vacation.

My last day with the staff I had come to love was a memorable one. Heidi being the motherly figure, made sure we did a staff lunch that was accompanied with a white elephant gift exchange. I was legitimately sad to leave my work family. I am sure most of you readers can relate. Work is a lot less stressful when you know you can count on your co-workers to not just be supportive, but also be friends at the end of the day. That's exactly what I had and I was willingly giving in up and walking into a new job that would take me down a path I had never experienced.

After a late lunch and mini-party, we said goodbye. This wasn't the last time I would see most of them. I was on my way back to Portland with my friend and some dude from craigslist rideshare who was super weird and creepy. It was on the drive back from Portland I got a ticket on christmas eve in a god forsaken place in Oregon called Baker City.

In Oregon it is illegal to pump your own gas. (As of 2018, it depends on the city you're in.) Driving at night presents a unique situation to have to deal with. 24 hour gas stations are not nearly as common as one would think. I was running low on gas so this can easily put you in a bind. Luckily we found one in Baker city. Or so we thought. I took the wrong exit and ended up on the east side of the city and not the west side like we needed to be. I made a wrong turn after wrong turn and ended up doing an illegal U-turn in front of a cop. The lights lit up and I said "god dammit."

The cop came up and informed me I had expired tags. (I planned on fixing that on this trip.) I made an illegal U-turn and did not signal my blinker. Fucking A. He took my license and after about 25 minutes, came back with a ticket. He decided to ignore everything, but the expired tags. I definitely deserved the ticket, but come on, man. It was christmas eve and I was trying to make it back home. Mercy would have been great in this situation.

When I finally arrived home, I was reunited with my best friend, Felipe. When Felipe gets excited she cries and almost barks in an excited tone, as most dogs do. I came home and her sister Lucy (RIP) clearly knew it was me since she was not barking. I went to say hi to Lucy but she was sleeping and her growl showed her disapproval of me bothering her.

My older brother whom at the time, I had discontinued any relationship with was living at home. That morning, my brother came home drunk from the night before. I could smell the Alcohol spewing from his mouth as he drunkenly told me he was wrong and how he wanted to make changes. This isn't the first time he had done this. This had become a regular occurrence when we began talking again or had any type of contact. Until recently, the contents of those conversation were always the same. he would apologize, tell me he's changing his ways, and then enlightens me on his newfound philosophy that if I don't embrace it I won't be nearly as happy as him. It's was the same shit that at that time, I couldn't care less to hear anymore than the times before. Things are very different now, but at the time, that's how they were.

The sweet reunion though was between my friends. The next night we all got drunk. This took me back to when we were in high school. My friends are fucking awesome. Out of everyone whom this very book is dedicated to, I met Jared first. The night I met him was during the summer going into my sophomore year of high school. That night, for whatever reason, I thought I was invincible and tried to jump a bench only to fall face first and act like I wasn't in pain. I was sore for a week. Jared went to school in Boston and received a degree in screenwriting. Jared is easily one of the best people I've ever met.

I met Jon my first day of sophomore year of high school. We both went to the wrong class and sat there for an hour and a half just talking and shooting the breeze. My first day at Westview High School was also Jon's. Neither of us knew anyone, so we decided we'd have lunch together that day since we literally didn't have anyone else to have lunch with. Mine and Jon's friendship has wavered at times, but all in all he is someone I'll always find myself missing.

I actually don't remember the first time I met Justen, or as Jared and I call him, Chusten. Apparently though I was an asshole to Justen, which I don't remember, but it wasn't until post high school that Justen and I became close friends. Justen in one of two people in my friends group I'll open up and tell everything to. He is usually my first call when I need advice. Justen is easily one of the hardest working people I've ever met. He paid his way through college despite coming from an almost destitute background and is currently working his ass off in the film industry.

Daylynn stands a solid 4'11. The first time I met Daylynn is a great story. We were swimming and something happened where she fell to the deep end and had to grab for something. I was right next to her. Her hand accidentally went into my swim shorts. That was the first time I had really any contact with her. That it the most psychical contact her and I have ever shared.

I met Branton through Jared. Branton also rode my bus. and lived in the neighborhood behind me. Mine and Branton's friendship was shaped through a mutual love for it's always sunny in Philadelphia, pissing off Jared and later on drinking copious amounts of alcohol in Eugene. Branton was in the Air Force and did not enjoy it.

Miranda is interesting. I met her separate of everyone else even though she knew them and even hung out with them. Her and I had two classes together sophomore year of high school and that's when we became friends. Funny story about Miranda and I. One time we went hiking in the Columbia river gorge, which is easily one of the most beautiful places in the country. We got the perfect type of high. Not too debilitating, not too light. As we began hiking, we were in way over our heads. Our highs wore off, our breathing intensified as it started raining, we began to question why we didn't bring the bud we had with us. Rookie move.

To say I love my friends is an understatement. I am forever thankful for my group of high school friends who have stood by my side whenever shit has hit the fan, which had happened multiple times since moving to Salt Lake City.

My trip to Portland was short. Shorter than what I wanted it to be. Once again, I had to say goodbye to Felipe, ugh. Saying goodbye to her is never easy. I'm thankful I was able to make it back home to Portland though. I really underestimated how much I missed my mom, dad and even my crazy little sister. The drive home was not anything I was prepared for, whatsoever.

The drive back to Utah generally takes about 10-12 hours. This drive would take me 18 hours because of the weather. I had never driven in heavy snow before.

It doesn't snow very often in Portland and when it does, the whole city shuts down. Though, give it a week and it'll be back to a constant rainy, drizzly overcast state.

The drive wasn't really bad at all until I hit the Blue mountains of Eastern Oregon. During the winter of 2014 the Rocky mountain range was experiencing an Unusually dry winter.

Park City, Utah which is notorious for skiing, and snowboarding had one of its worst years on record. That was until December 28th, 2014 when the whole region from Eastern Oregon all the way through Idaho, on down to Provo received their first true snowstorm of the season. This was also the day I was driving back to Salt Lake City.

Once I passed Pendleton, Oregon I was able to look ahead at the road I would be traveling, I was able to see plenty of snow.

I have a personality flaw that I use in certain cases such as this. I hide the reality of the situation through trying my best to be optimistic. This does not always work as well as I plan.

As I approached the first hill that leads to the pass, I attempted to veer right with the road, but instead, I kept going straight because I was in a 1996 Toyota corolla with bald tires. I ended up in a field of snow and no way to get out. I tried to drive but nothing happened. My failed attempts only yielded the smell of burning rubber.

I began shaking at this point. I had driven already for about five and half hours, so turning back and waiting for the storm to pass was not an option. Not only was I shaking, but I was also tired and sleep deprived. After about half an hour, a service vehicle saw me and shoveled me a path out. Thank God for that unnamed city worker.

At the top of the mountains is what is referred to as Deadman's Pass. Deadman's Pass is accurately named. The name of the pass has been reinforced over the years through several accidents. With numerous car accidents and fatalities every year due to the weather as well as drivers who don't realize the carefulness needed to drive through the pass, the name has proven to be accurate.

As I miraculously, but slowly climbed to the top of the pass, while in the thick of it, I noticed I had an eighteen wheeler in my blind spot to the right of me, I looked over to my left and there was a cement barrier. I turned up the music to help calm my nerves.

Every so often I would look over at the semi truck next to me and notice it would shake ever so slightly. This continued for about a mile. I was going roughly about 20-25 mph in near white out conditions. I looked over and was able to see the semi- truck's bed coming into my lane. I honked and yelled every profanity, but it was all in vain. All I could do was try best to keep control of my car. The semi-truck sideswiped me. I can easily remember envisioning myself being smashed between the barrier and the truck. The truck, I doubt, felt itself sideswiping my car. It kept barreling down the pass. I didn't even care that I had not gotten the driver's information. I was just happy to be alive. I was lucky that day. The semi-truck had one of those beds used for transporting heavy construction equipment. This meant the cargo load of the eighteen wheeler was lowered. If it had been one carrying traditional freight, my car probably could have been caught underneath and this incident may have ended very differently.

After that happened I pulled over because chains were mandatory at this point. I was 99 percent sure I had chains in my trunk. I pulled over and collected myself for about ten minutes. I did not talk or even move. I was only processing what had just happened. I called my mom and only as moms can do, said "well you have no choice but keep going."

I opened my door to the frigid 20 degree weather, with snow blowing in every possible direction. I checked for my chains in my trunk and much to my dismay, I did not have any. Fuck. What was I to do? I stayed in the right lane and prayed the whole way through. I'm not a praying man, even when I was active LDS, but there's an old saying that says you'll never meet an atheist in a fox hole.

I made it through the pass scathed and ready to be done only to hit the 7 mile

downgrade. I nearly shit my pants at this part. While on the downgrade, I hit a piece of ice that shifted my car at most, five degrees to the right. There was nothing I could have done to correct the angle. I was heading straight for a snowbank and I was helpless. I missed a mile marker by probably two inches as my car slammed into the snowbank. My car, I'm sure, was at a 45 degree angle. Once again, I sat there in shock and disbelief. I was looking out my windshield at a pile of snow that my car was stuck in. I did not know what to do. Eventually, I called a tow company. I described where I was at and they dispatched a driver. I had no idea how I was going to pay for the tow out. I had about $100 to my name. After probably an hour, a man in a truck stopped and towed me out. He will never know how thankful I was for him.
I reached the city of La Grande, Oregon glad to be out of the pass. It was about noon at this time and I hadn't eaten since about four in the morning. I didn't feel hungry because of the adrenaline that was still rushing through my veins. The shakiness of my body wouldn't allow me to feel hunger. I attempted to eat, but I ended up throwing away a full meal because I wanted to get this drive over.
My joy of being through the worst was short lived. As I continued to drive I-

84 south into southern Idaho I could easily see another storm on the horizon. I thought "Fuck, here we go again." In meridian, Idaho, I picked up a friend of a friend. I would not be continuing this drive alone. On the drive, we talked and talked. This was mostly to pass the time and help keep my mind off the horrible driving conditions.

As we entered Northern Utah, the conditions began to worsen and it was now dark outside. The sun had set and so to, any confidence I had with getting through the rest of this drive unscathed.

We passed the last gas station within 50 miles, this was done on accident. I needed gas, but I was so out of sorts, I didn't even think about getting gas because I was so preoccupied with the road conditions.

We finally arrived in the Salt lake valley around 10pm. I dropped my friend off with her friend. Tired and exhausted, I called Rob, who was my now former co-worker. Rob had an apartment downtown and the last thing I was going to do was drive another 40 minutes out to Tooele. I would be staying the night at Robs. First thing we did was run to the local grocery store and get some beer and hot pockets. That thrown together meal was exactly what I needed.

Rob and I kicked back and watched some "It's always sunny in Philadelphia." This may not sound like much but, for me, it meant a lot. I hadn't just casually drank a beer and watched TV with a friend in Utah yet and to finally be able to be so casual with a new friend in a new city meant that it was all going to be alright because I had a growing support system and at the end of the day what more can you ask for? Rob still is a great friend of mine. More with him, later.

The next day I began my new job at the historic apartment complex, the Covey. The Covey itself was built in, I believe 1908. The Covey consisted of four building in total. Of course the already mentioned Covey, as well as the Meredith, Buckingham, and the largest one of them all, the Hillcrest. All four buildings were once beautiful and timeless until neglect happened which, is common when different management groups come in and change out over the years. Certain things just get lost and in this case the Covey had lost its beauty in many aspects.

The staff at the Covey are some people of the best people I had met in Utah as well as some of the best Coworkers I have ever had. As mentioned before, Cricket was the business manager. Cricket stood a solid 5'7, but had the attitude of someone who was 6'7. Cricket was a tough lady and didn't take shit from anyone. As stern and blunt as she can be, she can turn right around and be very sweet and caring. Cricket was the type of manager that you would allow you to go into her office, sit in a chair, let out a deep sigh and vent while she asked "what's wrong sweetie?' My time working with cricket was too short, but I loved it. She would end up leaving a month later. Before she left I told her "I felt robbed" that I didn't get to work with her for a longer period of time.

Rob (different rob) worked on the maintenance side of the property. He had tattoos all over his body, including a small cross below his right eye. Looking at Rob, it was safe to assume he'd been through some experiences that I could not have imagined. That was a safe assumption I would learn later on.

Rob Would give me so much shit that it didn't really matter what I said he would disagree and make me look like I had no idea what I was talking about. Despite this, Rob is one of the most trustworthy people I know. He is a badass who works hard for his kids.

My main trainer on the leasing side of things was Bianca. Bianca was a tough lady who had grown up in a rougher part of a city called Ogden, which is about 45 minutes north of Salt Lake City. Bianca had been doing property management for about two years by the time I was hired. To say she knew just about everything is an understatement. She had so much patience when it came to training me that If I was training someone such as myself, I'd probably quit before my second week because I could not handle it. Bianca was also motivated to work hard for her child. Bianca would always talk about her child in a way only an adult can talk about the most important person in her life. Bianca was the company's best leasing agent and she knew it. Not in a cocky or pretentious kind of way, but if she needed something, or pushed the envelope a little bit she knew she would get away with it. Very quickly Bianca and I created this bond of covering for each other. I won't divulge this information because that would break the trust.

The assistant manager was Jourdan. Jourdan had been in property management since she had graduated high school and was a business manager herself previously in her employment with the company. She was doing her best to keep her crumbling family together which often meant sacrificing her own happiness. Jourdan would often vent to me in the months following. She was angry with her personal life as well as her work life. The property Jourdan was a manager at, had switched management groups. When that happened, Jourdan lost her title. She was offered the job of assistant manager at the Covey with the hopes of regaining her previous position at another property. One thing stood in her way and that was the same regional manager that interviewed me, Spencer.

I had finally found an apartment downtown. I found the apartment during the renovation of the Meredith. When it was time for my lunch I would walk down first avenue toward temple square, on my way to city creek mall. I loved being downtown. When I saw the illuminated sign that said Castle Heights, I instantly fell in love. I looked at it the next day. I envisioned myself living there. I put down my deposit a week later. Though, it would be another month and a half before I would move in. It was at 1st avenue and A street. It was less than a block away from the Covey, which was perfect. It was also three blocks away from my first apartment in Salt Lake City. It was a 200 sq ft. studio, and I was in love with it.

Eagerness to move out of Tooele as well the stress of starting a new job was interesting. I would spend my days learning a new job and taking on all the emotions that come with that, like worrying whether your co-workers like you, getting mad at myself and of course wondering if my next screw up would be my last. On the drives back to Tooele I would think about how much I hated having to drive out there. I wouldn't get home sometimes until 7:45-8 when I got off at six. At home I would eat my pizza rolls and drink mountain dew while tending to my tinder account.

Three days before I moved from Tooele to my apartment several very important things happened. The amount of driving I did in my first three months was staggering. It was at least 50-60 miles a day on my car and some days it would be closer to 100.

The Friday before I moved was like any other day. I woke up got ready for work and began the 40 minute drive to the Covey. The morning was nothing out of the ordinary. As I was driving, I distinctly remember listening to the song 60 ft tall by the dead weather when I heard a crack that had to have taken place somewhere on my car. The crack felt as if it had originated from my pedals. As I thought "Oh, that was weird" About two seconds later, white smoke began pouring out from under my hood like there was no tomorrow. I instantly knew this was bad.

I pulled over the side of the road and tried to convince myself that if I turn my car off then back on it'll all be fine. I turned my car off and called a mechanic back in Tooele. I was only about three miles outside of Tooele. I asked the mechanic if they could take a look at it. The mechanics response was "if you're lucky enough to get it here." That did not help my devastation. I was praying and sincerely hoping my car would be okay. This was my first car, it was my baby. It's name was Heisenberg. Yes, from Breaking Bad. This car did whatever it wanted to, much like Walter White. I turned my car on and it trembled and shook like nothing I had ever felt before. I flipped a U-turn and headed back to Tooele. As I approached the intersection of Erda way and UT-36, Heisenberg turned off for the last time and died as I was turning right to avoid being in traffic. I sat in the middle of the road blocking the rest of traffic. Rather than people asking me if I needed help, they honked and yelled at me. Why the hell do people do this? Yeah, I just want to fucking sit in the middle of the intersection. No, dumbass. After about five minutes some good ole country boys helped me push my car into a nearby store as I waited for a tow truck. I got out to say thank you, but they were gone as quick as they appeared.

Totaled was the diagnosis. the engine was done. That morning, I rented a car and went into work. Little did I know this wouldn't be the worst of my car troubles.

I had a lot to look forward to though. I was moving into my own place in three days, and later that night I had a

Tinder date with a beautiful girl named Abigail who would take me on an emotional roller coaster like no one else previously had. I moved into my apartment on January 19th, 2015. Moving from Tooele wasn't very hard at all. The hardest part has been what has taken place overtime. Matt and I don't really talk anymore and it's a damn shame. It could be for a number of reasons. Maybe living together soured the friendship? Maybe our friendship depended on my activity in the church? Maybe we're not as good of friends as I thought we were? Regardless, I miss my friend. I texted him some weeks later after I had moved into my apartment to see how he was doing. The response was a cold hearted "good." I took that as a hint that that was all he cared to say and even that, he forced himself to say.

Life's a pain in the ass that way. The people you grow with the most, are often the first ones to leave. I've learned people come as fast as the wind in a storm and leave before you can even put your coat on. Even the ones you love most and think of as family, will leave eventually and at the end of the day, If you're not content with sitting alone in your apartment by yourself then you will need to fix things.

I've had to learn and relearn this several times. Whenever we become

content it's easy to forget what we've learned. Re-learning is when you truly progress and learn more about yourself because if you don't, you're sacrificing your happiness.
My experience in Tooele taught me a lot about myself. It taught me the church isn't what I want in my life. Although I would struggle with this for another 6 months, Tooele pushed me closer to total withdrawal from the church, which I had never truly considered. It taught me that If this move was going to work, I would need to get used to people leaving my life and having to deal with it by moving on by myself. I learned that it's okay to rely on people for help as long as you are working to stand on your own. As god forsaken as Tooele is, I'm thankful for the three months I spent there.

Abigail Chapter 3

Oh gosh, where to begin with Abigail. I mentioned In the previous chapter, I had met Abigail on Tinder. At one time, I would have been embarrassed about admitting my use of Tinder. Now with tinder, as well as online dating, in general being so accepted, I no longer fear talking about it. The thing that is so interesting about tinder, is in society we often taught not be shallow and instead look for someone who has a heart of gold and will help you be the best person. Society (mainly millennials) love to post pictures and motivational type meme's or comments to the context of just that. There seems to be a call for originality, individualism and the willingness to let freedom of expression be free of the oppression of judgements, hateful comments, and even the shallowness of one's looks. Yet, this also coincides with Tinder's popularity. You be the judge.

I personally think society will slowly begin to adopt the standard it is going for. I'm no exception though, I would like to think that I am perfect when it comes to giving people the lack of judgements they want, seek and deserve but i'm not. I'm sure most of you can relate when I say I've sat in my bed at two in the morning swiping aimlessly. Abigail was and still is absolutely gorgeous. At that time, she was a couple years younger than me. However, she was light years more intelligent than I was. She was smart, beautiful, funny and cultured. She stood about 5'0 tall and had short blonde hair. If she was a model in the 60's, she could have easily kept up with Elizabeth Taylor and Audrey Hepburn.

She had the personality of an eastern European philosopher post WWII. She had more books than I had ever seen a peer of my own have. Her books ranged from Shakespeare to Bukowski and every major philosophical writer of the past 200 years. She loved browsing book shops and finding pieces of literature that she could find to add to her collection. This was just as exciting to her as you or I might find shopping for new clothes, or other slightly more worldly things. She thrived on education and a love of all things pertaining to literature.

As of now, my go to music is very roots rock, folk and blues. This would have happened at a much slower pace if Abigail hadn't enlightened me on such music. She introduced me to a world of music that I was just the beginning to enter. At the time, I loved Bob Dylan and Neil Young. There were a couple other bands and artists from around that time, but for the most part I listened to modern indie/folk.

On our first date, I felt rather foolish. If you may remember, this was also the same day my car had died, so I was picking her up in a rental. Sounds nice, until I realized I had to tell her this was not the standard of living I was at in my life, or she would naturally find out that it was not. I had just come from work, so I was still in my casual friday work clothes. When I go out on dates, like most, I try to look presentable, but on this date I did not look the way I wanted to because I couldn't. I had my brown work

boots, with an old pair of jeans, a black long john style shirt that had in big bold letters my company's name on it. I almost felt embarrassed because I did not think I was going to make the kind of impression on her that I wanted.
This wasn't because Abigail had any expectations, but rather, it's a reflection on my insecurities as a person. Throughout my life I had struggled with thoughts of inadequacy. I stand 6'2, but it is easy for me to feel 5'2 when around people I feel are more put together and more accomplished than I am.
Regardless, I was thirsty for social interaction and if it was to come from a tinder date, then so be it. I began to have the pre-date jitters. I had been on numerous dates at this point in my life, but not all were accompanied by this feeling. When this feeling occurs, at least in my case, it is because there will be more than an initial date. It's essentially my gut telling me there is more to what will be transpiring.
I left work and drove to pick Abigail. She lived near the University of Utah. When I arrived, I put the car in park and anxiously awaited her to join me. The pre-date jitters turned into a pounding heart and sweaty palms. Abigail's silhouette appeared in the doorway that led out of her apartment

building. She was even more gorgeous in person.

As she opened the door and climbed into my car, my thought was "why does she want anything to do with me?" I did what I do when I get nervous. I talk too much and begin to switch to all sorts of different topics like it's nobody's business. The plan was to grab dinner, then go hangout with some of her friends.

The outcome of the night is nothing I would have ever anticipated or expected, but only in my wildest dreams. I have never been the one to have a silver tongue, or be able to attract beautiful women such as Abigail. It's just not who I am.

we had about a 5-10 minute drive to chipotle, (hell yes, Chipotle.) Anyone who has met anyone from Tinder can probably relate to the first few moments being awkward and not knowing how to progress the conversation. This was definitely the case for me.

I really can't remember exactly what was said but I don't look back and remember the awkwardness as much as I remember the lack of an uncomfortable feeling. Abigail was naturally a very friendly person, so this feeling was never an issue because she accepted me for everything I was.

In reality, I was a shy, timid and shaky in the knees at best, newly turned 23-year old. My awkward, shy and cautious self hadn't tasted a sense of normalcy while in Utah. I was on the cusp of it.

Whenever I get excited about a girl I begin to fantasize about being together and begin to develop a crush and invest way more than the other person and this results in a lot of things not going my way. I fantasized about having my own apartment, dating this beautiful girl, succeeding at my job and being a more well-rounded person. I was so close to everything I could possibly want at that time, yet all I had to do was not be so fucking annoying by over talking. My memory is failing me when it comes to the dinner aspect of the date, but I love Chipotle so it couldn't have been too bad. After dinner, we went back to Abigail's house since we had time to kill before we were to meet up with her friends. Back at her house we ended up talking for hours and exchanging music suggestions.

She lived on her own, in a basement apartment. It was a one bedroom that had pipes running through the living room. As aforementioned, her room was filled with books and records.

Abigail and I sat on her bedroom floor exchanging songs. This was an early 2000's Conor Oberst song come true. One of the songs that was played fully encapsulated the perfect range of emotions felt that night. The song was "something in the air" by Thunderclap

Newman. the band was assembled by Pete Townshend of The Who. though, not actually a member of the band, he played a huge part in the bands early success.

The song jumps around and has an amazing bridge. On later dates, Abigail and I would comment about how perfect the moment that song played moment was. After Abigail and I exchanged songs for about 45 minutes, we decided to watch something on Netflix. I didn't think this was "Netflix and chill." I didn't have that intention mostly due to my confidence. I haven't the slightest idea of what we watched, maybe house hunters? I remember her and I were sitting very close to each other. I had my hands resting on my thighs thinking that just maybe we might hold hands. As the show progressed, so did my willingness to not pay attention and instead, be more concentrated on her. Just as mine were, her hands were on her thighs, as if to send me the exact same message I was. Only she had more confidence than I did, clearly.

I was ever so slightly moving my hand closer to hers when her right pinky extended out and touched mine. I'm oblivious to a lot of things when it comes to the opposite sex, but I understood what she was doing. I held her hand and turned to look at her. We kissed for the first time right there on her couch.

Once again I won't go into detail. However, that night Abigail and I went to sleep embracing each other like we had been lovers for years. That morning I woke up to a beautiful girl that I really thought would be around for a long time. I did not stay for long because I had work the next morning, so I had to wake up early. I also wasn't sure how to act the morning after, so leaving early worked out great.
This was not a casual hook up. There was more to it for me. I drove back to Tooele with the thought on my mind of, what's next? I wanted to keep seeing her.
I quickly got ready and turned right around to make it to work. Abigail and I had made plans for the next night. This night was to be different though. My car was dead in a parking lot on the edge of Tooele. I was moving on Monday and was busy Sunday so that would be the night that I would say goodbye to my car.
After work, I picked Abigail up and we were off to Tooele. I was going back out there to change and say goodbye to my car. Our relationship went straight to a pre-determine the relationship feel, if you will, at least it did for me. There wasn't really any awkwardness at all, there was even comfortable silence. For me, this usually takes a while to create that type of depth in the relationship. We arrived at the

shop so I could say goodbye to my car. I loved this car, after all it was my first car.

I bought the car when I was 21. It was my baby. I never let anyone else drive it. I named it Heisenberg, because that car would do whatever the fuck it wanted to. I knew this would be hard but I was going to try to keep it together since Abigail was to be joining me.

As I approached my car for the last time and sat in the driver's seat Abigail joined me in the passenger seat.

Driving when I had more to drink than one should, long drives home after a blown date, and aimless drives with friends were the memories that began to flood my mind.

I wasn't alone though. I said goodbye to so many things that happened in my life because of that car, Abigail put her arms around me as the tears began to flow. (There were many.) We spent about 5 minutes embracing each other as I said goodbye to such a pivotal piece of machinery. If it had not have been for that car, I wouldn't have ever made it to Utah. As silly and trivial as it sounds to be this torn up over a car, it what that car represented that caused the emotion behind my reaction. That car represented my hard work. I bought that car by working part-time as a courtesy clerk at a grocery store. I walked 1.6 miles to work everyday so I can take out trash, bag groceries, gather carts, and perform whatever other chore was asked of me. I would then walk 1.6 miles home. There were times I would get off at 10PM and have to open at 7AM. I busted my ass for that car. I can't leave out the people who sold me the car. The Hinton family made this possible.

After about 5 minutes of Abigail comforting me, I asked to be left alone one last time with Heisenberg. Abigail obliged and went back to the rental car. I bawled like a baby. I sat there and thanked my car while I wiped away the tears from my cheek. I thanked Heisenberg for helping me get to the Salt Lake valley. I thanked Heisenberg for all the memories.

I thanked Heisenberg for helping me realize I'm capable of doing hard things as long as I had the right tools at my disposal. Puffy eyed and red-faced, I got out and walked back to the rental car.

Abigail embraced me with a hug and a kiss on the cheek. At least I had that going for me. I would spend the night at her house again that night. This would be a continuing trend. While I was ready to be in a relationship with Abigail, there were several obstacles that made me think this was likely to not be a reality.

Abigail had dated a man by the name of Kevin. Kevin was a really good guy whom I to this day, think very highly of. Abigail and Kevin had dated all throughout high school and at that time, had recently broken up with in the past year. She considered him one of her best friends.

She had also mentioned to me about another guy she had been involved with. I was never able to get his name. however, later, I believed he was actually not a reason for her distance, but rather an excuse. Abigail would continue to use tinder around me. I had deleted tinder about a week and a half into mine and Abigail's romantic involvement because I was convinced she was my reason to delete it.

Abigail unintentionally did several things that persuaded me to give her the benefit of the doubt, however, It was a very confusing time for me. For example, while I was at work I was texting Abigail and had mentioned I was feeling rather sleepy.

In the early days of our relationship, feeling sleepy was a constant because of the nights we spent trading off at each others apartments. While at work, she appeared before me, in my office with a red bull in hand.

I was humbled and excited to see her. I introduced her to Cricket, Bianca and Jourdan. I am not used to people doing nice things for me. Maybe that is why I fell for her so hard and out of control.

As I write this chapter, the very light that illuminates my room, comes from a lamp she gave me. The table which I would share many conversations with her and drinks with others, had been purchased by her. She never asked for any money in return, nor would she accept payment.

I was confused though. Frequent calls back home to Daylynn were a desperate plea for help. She would try her best, but her efforts can only go as far as I do when it comes to accepting the reality of my situation. The reality was we would get high, watch netflix and have sex. Is this to say that she wasn't as emotionally invested as I was? I believe at times she was very emotionally invested, but that wavered day-to-day.

Super Bowl Sunday 2015 was what I thought would be the nail in coffin when it came to her being as emotionally wrapped up as I was. Abigail's family hosts a party every year on the Superbowl between her and Kevin's family. Abigail invited me because she wanted me to meet her family and she knew I was a football fan. I reluctantly agreed.

I was reluctant because these families were very close, then here I was, not related to anyone, attending and stuck in the middle.

The car ride to Alpine, Utah, where Abigail was from, was about 30-45 minutes. The whole drive I would eagerly ask questions to get a better feel of the situation. I was not prepared for the awkwardness of what was to transpire. It was to be Kevin's family watching the super bowl with Abigail's family.

We arrived. I could feel my awkwardness and quietness begin to show. I nervously stayed near Abigail. Abigail became very nostalgic as we walked the halls of her childhood home. She told me stories of times she came home drunk and high. She showed me her beloved instruments and records that laid in the corner of her old childhood room. I began to realize even more this was the girl for me.

Though, my inner desire was to drink and rid myself of the feelings of this evening, my pride wouldn't let me embarrass myself by drinking too much. after about 15 minutes of Abigail and I talking about her childhood, the doorbell rang. It was Kevin's family. Awesome. Nothing against Kevin or his family, but I was in such an uncomfortable situation. All I could do was blush out of embarrassment. Abigail was very good friends with Kevin's sister, so they ran off together. All four adults went downstairs to watch the game, leaving me with Kevin and her brother. What the fuck was happening? Kevin and Abigail's brother are very close, so they sat at one end of the couch, me at the other. As much as this sucked, I was happy to be watching the game. The game itself acted as an escape. Something I could watch to occupy me. The Seahawks were trying to repeat as super bowl champs, but came up short against the patriots. I hated this whole situation.

It was one of those situations that when you're in the midst of it, you think to yourself "how did I end up here?" I saw Abigail during the course of the game 2 minutes at most. Kevin and her brother were having a grand ol time and I couldn't wait for the game to be over.

When the game was over I put on a fake smile and shook everyone's hand and acted jubilant that I was there. The car ride back with Abigail was not any better.

Abigail and mine's brief time together was marred by what we wanted for the long-term. I wanted a relationship, she said she wasn't sure what she wanted. We would have this conversation from time to time with the same conclusion. "Let's not worry about it now."

When Abigail and I got into the car, she became very quiet and reserved. I tried my hardest to get her to speak to me and open up, but thinking back on it if she had, it was because she felt a connection strong enough to think I can help her resolve her deep and intimate personal issues. I was right to think something was lacking.

We arrived at Abigail's apartment with the same uneasy silence that accompanied us on the drive home. We entered her apartment and immediately sat on the couch.

I asked her what was going on. I broke into my usual pre-serious discussion which is essentially me beating around the bush.

Abigail finally spoke about what was on her mind. Thinking back on this time, I can't help but wonder if this was a made up situation so she can paint the picture for me that she was not ready for a relationship and instead of having to let me down, I would draw my own conclusion about her mental capacity to handle a long-term relationship at this time in her life.

She spoke of a boy whom she had once been seeing. (The one whose name never mentioned to me.) She told me her longingness to be with him. He had a choice, she almost excruciatingly told me what they were. Not that he was necessarily being pushed into one or the other, but more so, he had options. He had Abigail, whom from what I gathered from this conversation, was absolutely wrapped around his finger. It was to the point that Abigail would not go to some of her favorite places

because they had gone to these places and the knowledge that she could not be with him was enough to scar her so deep that she avoided some of her once favorite places. Going there with him created an associated memory for her. The other option for this mysterious man was the one he would ultimately take, which was getting back together with his ex-girlfriend.
I do not know this man nor do I know his ex. However, I will say this. He found himself having to choose. I didn't need to choose. I already knew who I wanted, I wanted to be with Abigail. This man went with his ex. This devastated Abigail. I was the rebound. I found out that night I was not what Abigail wanted. I was temporary, at best. I was not going to be the one she was going to love or the one she would seek solace in after a long day. I was not going to be the one that can shake her every nerve and fear just by simply being myself around her. The person who could have done that was someone else. Someone that did not feel the same way that I felt about her. This realization began at that time but would not set in until a couple of weeks later. Our bickering ended and we fell asleep together on her couch holding each other in a very fake way that only those that retreat into a pseudo-optimistic emotional state do

because, if only for a couple more weeks, to delay the inevitable.

As time went on, our conversations about the future became almost daily. I tried to be optimistic and think "well it'll work itself out, and we be together here soon." She began to tell me she did not want a relationship. She mentioned her new medication was making her horny. This bothered me, though I may be wrong, but it almost seemed to be her way of excusing the lust and emotion behind have us having sex.

I basically ignored this and tried to be optimistic about the whole situation until one day. Abigail said it would be best if we did not talk for a week. My heart was shattered. The ending had been written on the wall the whole time. I just chose to ignore it, thinking and even accepting my fantasy of a resolution as reality in waiting. Even during the week we didn't talk, I had high hopes as to what the outcome might be. My hopes were that after a week she would come back and it would all be over.

What would be over would be our daily conversations about or relationship status because we would be in a relationship.

My anxiety and stress ran high as the week passed. Abigail was my every thought. Every song I listened to brought back vivid memories of the romance Abigail and I shared. She was

in everything I did during that week.
We texted briefly and she agreed to
come over that following friday.
We sat at the table she had bought for
me while the light from the lamp she
gave me illuminated her pale skin, blue
eyes and the rest of her beautiful
features.
I began to speak.
I told her I was going crazy not being
about to talk to her about how my day
was going. I told her how often I
thought about her and missed the smell
of her hair. I missed our nights
lounging around and watching house
hunters.
As our conversation strayed to other
topics, she held my guitar and began to
play the classic "it ain't me babe" by
Bob Dylan. I swear on my life that how
she began to tell me that this wasn't
going to work.
As she began to explain why she was not
seeking a relationship, she stopped
playing guitar and looked down. She had
a look of deep contemplation on her
face. she uttered the words "I'm just
having fun being single right now." She
made it seem like it was a hard
decision and one that was agonizing to
make. After our conversation, she
invited me to go to the grocery store
with her. While we were there, we would
try to restrain ourselves from holding
hands and kissing. We both told each
other we will be friends and whatever

happens, happens. I was hopeful moving forward. This was February 2015. I told her I would ask her in February 2016 if she was ready for a relationship.
I never asked her.
We had made plans to begin our new stage of friendship but those quickly fell through when I reached out to her to confirm some plans we had made. She never got back to me.
I learned a lot from my limited time with Abigail.
Abigail dropped me off back home. It would be a year and a half before I saw her again. Some months later, she texted me saying she had heard "Something thing in the air" and she had thought about me.
When we saw each other, we grabbed coffee, caught up and even spoke of past relationships we had been in since our time together. We played guitar, laughed and ate. I never saw her again. When things ended with Abigail, I learned how truly lonely I was. Abigail was really the only person I was actively friends with in Utah. I didn't have anyone I could go on a midnight stroll with to talk things over and just have peace of mind knowing I was able to confide with someone whom I called a friend. Abigail taught me to not get so emotionally wrapped up too early, because at any moment the rug can be swept out.

While Abigail and I were seeing each other, she would occasionally mention a guy whom I will call Raul. Raul was someone whom she had met through mutual friends.

One night we were at her apartment and had a craving for a burrito. Not strange, because her and I often smoked weed and would always make late night runs to get food. She texted Raul that night to bring her a burrito and to come hang out with us. I wasn't against this because of the lack of friends I had in my life. Raul came over and we all had a good time. I remember he came off as very pretentious, but all in all, a good guy. Abigail was fine with this, which meant by consequence, so was I.

In the months following mine and Abigail's fall out, I would often take walks around downtown Salt Lake City to think and just listen to music to clear my head. One night in particular, I was walking by my favorite cafe and could not help but notice Kevin sitting outside with his then girlfriend. I legitimately enjoyed seeing him and sharing a 10 minute conversation. He informed me that Abigail and Raul had been dating and were now in a relationship.

This news didn't surprise me. I had already accepted the fact that I was the rebound and Abigail had easily and rather quickly, moved on because she hadn't seemed to have invested as much emotion into it as I had.

My main concern was why couldn't she just have been honest? I posed this same question to Kevin's girlfriend and she said "Girls don't know if a guy's going to freak out on them." Very fair response. let's say that was the case, I was not a ticking time bomb. It just seemed like I was fed excuses to "protect" me emotionally. I can understand lying to protect yourself. But I thought Abigail and I were on a different level than a traditional excuse.

When the lie's unfold and the truth comes out, the hurt is 10 times worse should the person who lied had been honest in the first place. Second, it's not up to you to protect me.

If we don't want the same thing don't drag it out and try to use rudimentary manipulation to think I'll figure it out on my own, as was the case in this situation. Don't insult my intelligence like that. Third, Honesty will hurt, but only for a short time. It's the lies and deceit that can and really do fuck you up for a long time.

I will say one thing though, I firmly believe at one point Abigail really did care about me. As evidenced by the lamp, couch and even something like bringing me a red bull at work. I wasn't always honest with Abigail, though. I never really told her about

the internal struggle I was having with the church at this point in my life.
I hope abigail is doing well. I've spoken to her several times and she is still a great person. This was several years ago, so it's hard to judge someone when they're younger. I'm confident that if we were to see each other again, we would embrace each other as old friends do.
My backup plan if this whole Abigail thing did not work, was to attend church faithfully and turn a blind eye to all the "sinning" I had committed with Abigail. I convinced myself that this was a blessing from god as a means of turning my life around from going south. Thinking back on it, I did not want to accept the fact that I, as a person, was not the one Abigail wanted to end up with. I thought that by accepting a higher powers intervention, that I did not lack anything as a person, but the situation just was not meant to be. The truth was I lacked many things as a person and I needed to change.

Lonely Decision Time
Chapter 4

After things went south with Abigail, I really didn't know what to do. I went from having a great apartment, a beautiful girl and the excitement of moving to a new city, to the opposite end of the spectrum. Soon, all I had was the loneliness and depression that made doing anything more than the necessities seem like a waste of time. I didn't feel it was fair what had happened. It took me a long time to realize life, in general, is never going to be 100 percent fair. Fair is a term thrown around a lot, but it's all relative. There's really no way to know if the situation is fair because of our own biases.

So far, my move to Salt Lake City had not been fair to me and I did not realize at that time, life would get even more worse and rather than complaining about it, I quickly learned I was wasting time by wallowing in self-pity when I could be finding a resolution.

I have never been medically diagnosed with depression, nor do I even get close to saying I was depressed. I am not a huge fan of people that do that. It takes away from those who have truly suffered from such a terrible mental illness.

A lot of the way I describe it, is more of an optimistic approach. I describe it as just going through a funk. The reason for this is, because if I can convince myself it'll pass, then I can begin to look past it. Once again, I cannot say I know what it feels like to truly have depression. So if you suffer from depression, my strategy might not work for you. Just know, I'm rooting for you.

However, I felt I was on my way because of the lack of motivation I had to meet people, explore, work on my own happiness and make new friends. I was confused to say the least. I knew I needed to get out of this mental state though. I realized it was not healthy. At this point, I was car-less and with my tax return fast approaching, I decided it was time to truly explore Utah. I was in the beginning stages of what felt like depression and I knew it was not where I wanted to be.

Growing up before my parents hit financial difficulties, my dad had a 2000 Jeep Cherokee sport. I have fond memories of riding in that car while my father played his favorite band, The Beach Boys. When things got hard, my dad had to trade it in for a late eighties Saab.

It took me several years before I realized I lived in ignorance to the things my father did for me, my mother and siblings. My father and I do not have the best relationship. As mentioned before, my parents split when I was fourteen and I was too much of an angsty teenager blasting my Brand New and My Chemical Romance to realize this. I convinced myself I had all the problems often found in lyrics with-in the "Emo" Genre. I really did not. It was just easier to cry for pity and not solve my problems. As I've gotten older, my ideology on family relationships have changed, but not my actions. I want to, but I just do not know how to be functional and be myself around my family.

I began to look for a new car. Specifically for a jeep. I loved the look of a mid nineties jeep. I became obsessed with owning one. I would search Craigslist daily in hope of finding my new baby. I also searched KSL, which is a essentially a regional Craigslist and it is not nearly as sketchy as Craigslist. I did not have a lot of money but I was determined to make this work.

The whole no ride and no friends thing did make for a difficult situation. Though, there was one way around this.

I had some friends from high school down south in Provo. Friends, that at one point, I was very close with, but as the common denominator left (LDS church,) so did the relationship.

One such friend is Patrick. Patrick and I went to high school together and were very close at one point. Patrick is very strong in the gospel. He served his mission in Japan and came back an even more devout member than before. After I had been baptized, Patrick and I were very close. I used to lean on him in times when Alcohol was around and I felt I wanted to be follow the teachings of the church.

After about a solid week of searching, I finally found the perfect jeep. (Or so I thought.) One evening, Patrick came up from Provo to help me out so I could acquire this car.

Patrick and I can really only agree on one band, and that is the aforementioned Brand new.

Brand new was as big of a part of my high school experience as any class I took, assembly I attended, or class I skipped. I saw them for the first time in concert My senior year of high school. This was to be my first true concert. Along with Brand New being my favorite band, Manchester Orchestra was a close second.

Manchester Orchestra had just released their sophomore album, Everything to nothing. Brand New had just released their fourth album, Daisy. If I was not listening to one, I was listening to the other. Even to this day, I still listen to both albums from time to time. Though, Manchester Orchestra broke my heart when they released "Simple Math." Not a fan.

The night I saw them in concert was one of the best nights of my life. Nothing could have prepared me for seeing those two bands. In attendance were, Jared, Patrick, Blair and this girl named Kylie, who at the time, was best friends with my then girlfriend. When

Brand new played "seventy times seven," I could have died happy at that moment. I've seen brand new twice since then, but nothing can compare to the first time.

The Jeep was beautiful. It was a 1996 forest green Jeep Cherokee sport. It was lifted and looked like it was able to handle everything Utah could possibly throw at it. Patrick picked me up and we were off.

We arrived at possibly one of the sketchiest looking apartment complexes in the state of Utah. I met the seller who looked rough around the edges, but seemed like an all around good guy. I wanted a vehicle and this was the easiest way to get it. I test drove the jeep and definitely ignored some key warning signs. The breaks were awful, it had a cable coming from underneath the center console with an operational red button. This was used to kickstart the cars starter. I ignored all this because I wanted a vehicle and did not want to wait another second. I instantly fell in love, though I should not have. I bought my Jeep for $1,100. I named my Jeep after my favorite former NBA player. Rasheed Wallace.

Wallace is a badass dude. Wallace is the NBA's All-time leader in technical fouls. When I was growing up, the Portland Trail Blazers were known as the "Jail Blazers." They were constantly being arrested, mostly for marijuana possession. Portland loved them. I loved them.

This moment in my transition to Salt Lake City was definitely interesting. I found myself at ground zero. I felt trapped. I was unable to be social, even if I wanted to. I often would make plans thursday night that consisted of saying to myself "you know what, fuck it. I'm gonna go to a bar even if I'm by myself and see who I meet." Come friday night, I would stay inside my apartment and watch Netflix until I drifted off to sleep. There was no end to the lonely Fridays and even lonelier saturdays. It seemed to me, there was no end.

My days had been reduced to reminiscing about friends back home in Portland. Remembering good times that now seemed like a fleeting memory. I missed having something to do every weekend, I missed being able to text a friend and make plans, but most of all, I missed just having friends that are there whenever you needed them. This was easily one of the loneliest times I've had in Salt Lake City.

After thinking of solutions that I was too intimidated to attempt, I landed on one that took a lot of thought and consideration.

I decided I needed to go to church. I had already been going back to church, but I was only going through the motions. I needed to truly invest in the church. I needed to put myself out there and be around positive people. I needed social interaction with people whom I thought, but secretly knew, I couldn't relate too. I needed to attempt to connect with people whom I knew I could not be completely honest with.

I planned on attending church every Sunday, Monday activities and anything in between. I made this decision for two reasons: The first being that the church is all about love, acceptance and bringing everyone together, so why would I be an exception to that, right?

 The second being, I wanted to be active in the church, because I did still feel a semblance of accountability. Also, mentioned in the previous chapter, my thought process led me to believe that recent events was the act of God leading me back to the church.

The weekly congregation I attended was called the City Creek YSA, 1st ward. YSA is an acronym for "Young Single Adult." A YSA is a ward specifically designed for those in a younger age category; 18-30. The only qualification is that you cannot be married, since you would then be in a family ward, similar to the one I was in when I was baptized. However, those divorced, have kids, etc are able to attend, as well. The reason for the distinction is because of several reasons.

In a family ward, a lesson may be "rearing your children in the gospel." Not very applicable to a 23 year old just off his mission. The goal is to be around peers who are actively learning in the gospel, and preparing to go to the temple, serve a mission, get married, etc. All of what I mentioned is the hope. The reality and culture of the YSA is completely different, at least in my case.

What happens when you put a bunch of young LDS adults in a room? A high school simulation. The only difference, everyone is older.

The reality is it can be very clique, dramatic and immature. I sat by myself routinely at church. Church is three hours, mind you. In the ward I attended we had Elders quorum first.

Elders quorum is when all the men in the ward meet together to discuss things pertaining to men in the gospel. The church centers around what is called the "Priesthood." The priesthood is essentially the ability to administer blessings. Such as blessing the bread and the water, giving blessings of healing, and of strength, and others regarding the temple. Only men that hold the priesthood can baptize. The priesthood is also described in vague terms as a means to governing the "Lord's church." Most of the lessons have to do with "being a righteous priesthood holder."

Elder's quorum is an interesting place. People are not who you expect them to be. Some of the most pretentious people I've met are in an Elders quorum. In the church you're taught not to be worldly, yet some of these guys are wearing the latest and greatest suits with perfectly shined boots. It just struck me as odd. The lessons often contained messages about bringing the quorum together and feeling as one. If that was the case why was I never invited to sit with anyone? Why was I not being included in discussions? I will say this though, there were a couple of stand up guys who I believe exemplified what they believed.

Some of the greatest people I've ever met are active members of the LDS church, but by that same token, some of the least desirable people I've ever had the chance to even be in the same room as, were LDS, as well.

After Elders Quorum, the rest of church breaks down into essentially what is an audition. It is rudimentary flirting at its finest. Next is Sunday school. Sunday school is co-mingled and this is when a lot things become noticeable. The men would try their best to swoon the women. The basic flirting techniques would happen. I would take my seat in the back, then the lesson would start.

The lesson often time would take a story out of the bible or Book of

Mormon then as a class would dissect it and take certain aspects of it and "apply it to our daily lives." This is where the audition comes in. Guys, that in Elder's Quorum would routinely walk past me and not say a word would begin a lecture on how we all need to be doing things better and how we need to apply the "Lord's teachings" in our lives. Everyone would nod and approve. One thing has always bothered me in the church though, everyone is in a race for perfection, by default there really is no ground broke on issues that the average church goer might have. It was never a true discussion, as much as it was agreeing without hesitation.

Elder Henry D. Taylor, who at one point, was of the leadership of the church, said "Compliance to counsel without knowledge of the reason therefore is often referred to as "blind obedience. But obedience is not blind when it is based on faith-implicit, trusting faith."

Elder Taylor did not dismiss the thought that LDS people tend to go on blind faith. Instead, he merely defined it. He is very firmly saying if you believe in god and you believe the person who is telling you counsel is sent of God, then believe it. While I'm speaking on the rudimentary church level, this is the same logic used by Warren Jeffs, Jim Jones and other countless sect leaders. Why find out for yourself, when you can trust me? While I've never been ok with the idea of blind faith, I did prescribe to the idea while an active member of the church.

The reason I bring that up is because why ask questions? The person who asks questions is often looked at as someone lacking faith. It is not fair. Maybe it was me, but I never felt comfortable asking questions, even more so when you're sitting all alone and do not have the support system needed when making changes in your life.

The general consensus seems to be "well, it must be right because it is coming from the church, and the church is true. We should just believe it."

After Sunday school, was the most important meeting of the church- Sacrament meeting. The reason Sacrament is so important to the church is because it is the time when partaking of the bread and water take place. This is the time when our sins for the week are forgiven under the condition we truly "repented" from our transgressions. The process of forgiveness can range from a simple prayer to talking to a bishop. It depends on the severity of the sin.

I have such a hard time with this. If forgiveness is between you and god, why would speaking to a bishop even be in consideration? What does he have that god does not? This gray area that is created, becomes very prevalent. People in the church try to define repentance, but I feel most people cannot define exactly how to "repent." Yes, you can pray and ask for forgiveness but when do you need to speak to a bishop? Someone may tell you that if it is a sexual transgression you'll need to speak to the bishop, but someone may tell you it all depends on how you feel after you pray about it. On the subject of repentance, the letter of the law and the spirit of law intermingle so much so, that people often say "repent" but fail to realize how contextual it is to each situation. Repentance is different for each person because each person interprets the subject differently.

After the administration of the bread and the water comes the talks. The speakers are pre-selected and are given various topics weeks in advance. I've given so many talks in church, that public speaking does not bother me in any way, shape or form. Talks are interesting, I've heard some that are very faith building and thought-provoking, however, I've also heard ones that seem to drag on and do not really do much. The same rules of and audition apply here, as well. Someone is inevitably going to get up and try to impress someone of the opposite sex through their level of spiritually. While not always the case, it does happen more often, than not. It got old after a while. Sacrament was always very interesting. I sat in the back by myself most of the time and I was able to people-watch very well. This particular YSA was very clique. I was able to see the various groups and it reminded me of high school. It severely killed my motivation to continue to go.

People in the church often try to address this and say things to the context of "It should not matter, you're there to grow spiritually not to make friends." While that is true, the social aspect is important in the fact, that there are those moments when you have five minutes to kill before the next meeting and are aimlessly standing in the hall feeling as lonely as can be, yet you're surrounded by people on all sides. Then There are those times when you want to ask a question, but you fear you're alone in your inquiry. I'm reminded of a lyric by one of my favorite bands, Portugal. The man. "Sad inconsistencies we see, when you find yourself lonely but right next to me." If this lyric was applied to church, this would imply that people at church really did care about those sitting alone. If they did I never felt it. This is a past reflection, However, this did bother me to a larger extent. Not enough to draw me away quite yet. Whatever happened on Sunday, was in the past. I still had mutual on Monday evenings to look forward to.

While I had it my mind I would attend weekly, that was rarely the case. I always backed out because I didn't have anyone to really go with. Yes, you can go and hope to meet people but my social anxiety wouldn't let me do that. I remember I did put myself out there one time. I felt awful and lonely as ever once the experience was done.

For weeks, the members of the YSA had been talking up an event coming up. It was to be a talent show and social. I had time to mentally prepare myself for it, so I thought I would go. I had been personally invited by several people of the ward. No one that I felt particularly close to, but getting an invite is always nice.

The night of the talent show came and I decided I would attend. I showed up late on purpose, because if I decided to leave early no one would notice. I walked in during the talent show to a dimly lit gym, with all focus on the stage. I hastily found a seat close to the stage, but not next to some of the people who had invited me. I sat at a table with people I had never talked to, but I was opened to meeting new people. By open, I mean if they talk to me. At that time, I had a hard time opening up and starting a conversation with someone I didn't feel I had a reason to. When the show was over, I

went up and tried to talk to several people I had talked to in the past but nothing stuck.
They would always end up going back to their group of friends and leave me standing there awkwardly.
I walked hastily for what seemed like an eternity. I finally made my way back to my car with my tail between my legs and almost feeling embarrassed that I had even shown up and tried to open up to people.
I went for a long walk that night and really thought long and hard if this was the right thing for me.
I weighed the pros and the cons. The pros were that I was active in the gospel and that what was "really important." The cons included what had transpired that night. Was the growth in the gospel worth the social anxiety? The answer at that time? Yes. Not by a large margin, though. I decided I was going to stick with it. This night was early May 2015. I still had another month of being almost as active as possible. While that night really hurt me, I decided to look past it. The reason was because I convinced myself I was in it for the spiritual aspect. The social part was just as important to me, but in order for me to have the strength to continue, I needed to act like it was not. This way I would not feel so embarrassed and ashamed at what transpired.

Nothing changed that night. I still went to church, I would still feel nothing, I would still back out of going to mutual and I still did not gain anything from going to church. However, things were different. I went back to going through the motions. My commitment was shrinking almost weekly. I was in a rut early on in my move to Salt Lake City. I was not happy with my life. The feelings of depression began to set in, again. The feelings that Abigail was able to wipe away were back because of her. Friday and Saturday nights were unbearable for many reasons.

I would on occasion walk past the popular bars down the street from my apartment in the hopes I may see someone I recognized from the Covey and I would get an invite to hang out with them. This never happened, but I was always a little hopeful. This improved at certain points. I would occasionally go out with coworkers and things were steady, not great, but steady.

At this point the church was important to me because I convinced myself it needed to be important to me. I thought I needed religion at this point in my life. It began to dwell on me, the church was suppose to be helping me, long term, as well as short term. This wasn't happening. So why was I still investing time and the barest amount of energy in this? My constant back and

forth was beginning to take its toll, mentally.
Occasionally, I would drink, smoke weed and forsake everything the church taught me to make a priority. I would question my beliefs, yet go through the motions on Sunday. Why? I was putting myself through an unhealthy mental cycle like I had done before.
I was nearing an ending point. I couldn't keep torturing myself mentally trying to live up to standards I didn't believe or support. At this time, those standards, wouldn't amount to anything other than self-harm and fake repentance. This ending point would come in a matter of months. I was oblivious to the fact that I was seriously damaging myself mentally. A little bit before this, I had met a girl named Haley who truly expedited my way out of the church.

Haley
Chapter 5

Haley was a situation I should have never been in. If I had been smart and followed the advice of my friends, I would not have had my heart broken and my faith just might still be intact. She took a lot, left very little and by the time we were done, I was almost a completely different person. Haley and I met at the peak of my back and forth struggle with the church, she did, however, help me realize things in a different perspective. I'm thankful for the time her and I spent together, but I would not do it again.

Haley and I met how a lot of people do nowadays. Online. Before, I've mentioned tinder, the platform was different, but the premise is the same. Okcupid. Haley reached out to me first. I looked at my phone in a state of disbelief. Why would this beautiful, cultured woman want anything to do with me? We talked all day, messaging back and forth. I began to get excited, but tried to deny it to myself so as not to get too excited, because my hopes would most likely be crushed. Given that it was online dating.

Haley and I had already made plans to grab drinks later in the week and that was fine with me. I was just happy talking to someone that seemed interested in me. Haley messaged me and asked to meet that night, instead. She said, to the extent, "You seem like a person worth getting to know and I would love to get together sooner." We made plans to meet at a bar called the Green Pig in downtown Salt Lake City. My nerves began to set in ten-fold. We were to meet at 7pm. I got off work and walked the half-block home. I was so nervous because her and I seemed to have so much in common. These ranged from music, hobbies and even to a similar family situation. I was nervous

because I tend to blow it more often than not. I spent probably 45 minutes deciding on what I should wear.
I walked the five blocked to the bar from my apartment with more and more nerves setting in with each and every step. I planned on being late by about 5-10 minutes. I did not want to seen too eager, although, that was far from the truth. I made it to the bar and saw her sitting there with her back to the door. I was sure it was her.
I approached this stranger, soon to be acquaintance, friend, lover and back to stranger.
I sat down and ordered a drink. Not a strong one, which was surprising, given my heart rate. As we talked, our conversation flowed. She told me all about her life and I told her all about mine. The conversation took many turns. I remember several things we talked about, but a lot of it escapes my mind. Those are the best type of memories. The feelings that come rushing back are the feelings of opening up in a raw situation become what you remember most.
Living in Salt Lake City, the church is a subject that comes up fairly often. I lied completely about the church. I should not have. I led Haley to believe It was not a part of my life at all, but that was far from the truth.
Haley and I bonded over music and life not going our way, in general. We had

been there for several hours. By the
time we left, it was dark. We were
heading back to my apartment. We walked
up State st. on a warm, spring night.
During our short walk, our hands
brushed up against one another, several
times. The last time they did, they
didn't separate. As much as I knew I
shouldn't be rushing into things, I
knew that my reservations and
precautionary thoughts were to no
avail. I was going to rush into things
with Haley no matter what. I was
convinced she would be the exception.
It was on the Northwest corner of State
and 300th avenue where Haley and I had
our first kiss.

Back at my apartment, we made small
talk. Continued drinking, played songs
and danced. We settled in for bed that
night. We embraced each other and
shared intimate moments as we drifted
off to sleep.

The person sleeping in my bed had a
past that created the perfect storm.
When Haley and I grabbed a drink, she
had just moved back to Salt Lake City.
She had been back for no more than a
week. The reason she had come back was
because she had fallen out of love with
her boyfriend whom she had met while
previously living in Salt Lake City.
When she mentioned that, I knew in the
back of my head I should have been
careful. That is not how my life works,
though. She left California with her

mother, struggling to plan the next move in her life. She had been living out in the Bay area while her boyfriend worked at Facebook. She described their relationship as one that had fallen apart because he devoted too much time to work and personal projects. She elaborated that she had decided months before she moved she would be ending the relationship.

She had been in a situation I had never been in and because of that, I felt she was needing companionship. Not that she needed someone to help her through that fall-out, but I wanted her to know that was an option. I felt I could help her through her old relationship while creating a new one. I was already too deep to realize the flaws of my logic. Haley was not a fan of the church at all. She was very close with her family, which is part of the reason she had such a disdain for the church. She herself was not LDS, not even by birth. Her older sister was a member. Her mother and her mother's boyfriend were also LDS. So she had been around the church from a very young age. She told me stories of her sister growing up in the church and not feeling accepted. She elaborated on the controlling nature of the church when it came to young women. I agreed with her. Her mother was LDS and had been an "inactive" member of the church since she had married her father.

She told me her true disdain for the church but I rationalized it to personal experience, some of the things she mentioned, I had seen, but not personally experienced myself. Extenuating circumstances create your personal experience. I was on the inside looking out. My vision was clouded by my bias. Of wanting the church to be a factor in my life. Haley had grown up in southern California and did not identify with Utah. Her father, for a long time, had a very successful photography business specializing in portraits. To say she grew up a child of privilege, was an understatement. Haley had traveled all over the world and had lived the life that most people only dream of. Her life was made to be and end perfect, but depending on who you are, life works out the exact way you do not want it to. Haley was in a transitional period during this moment in her life. She didn't seem to have any passions and did not plan on going to school, or furthering her education. She didn't seem to want to follow anything, anyone or even create something anew. She was working as a server at a popular bar/restaurant called Whiskey Street. She was content with that, but I was not. Was I judging her? Or did I know she was capable of getting more out of life? It was definitely both, though,

regrettably, the former was a bigger deal for me.
Since I was judging her by what I saw others doing, I wanted her to have a better lot in life. While my goal was in the right place, my reasoning came out of a negative and selfish place. Either way, it did not matter to her. I would later find this out, but as of right now, she was still in my bed after only knowing her for 6 hours.
The person lying in my bed with me when I woke up, was someone who was not even a week's time out a long-term relationship.
The person lying in my bed with me when I woke up was someone looking for some sort of purpose in a time in her life when everything was rocky.
The person lying in my bed dispelled everything and convinced me we were met to be together.
The person lying in my bed with me was someone I thought was perfect for me.
The reality was, this time, the previous morning, I woke up and got ready to work unknowing of her existence.
The person lying in my bed was someone I should have avoided and saw the warning signs.
The person lying next to her was just as rocky and unsure about his direction in life as she was.
The next morning, I woke up and began to get ready for work. Haley stayed

asleep. I was ok with letting her stay there while I was at work. After all, I had just met the perfect woman, right? I got to work in a great mood. Rob began to question me relentlessly, because I was hardly ever this jubilant. I began to tell him about last nights excursion. He was skeptical from the beginning. He told me this was a bad idea, but I ignored him. One of the last things I mentioned was that she was still sleeping in my bed. His reaction was "What?? I hope all your shit is still there when you get off work!" I instantly trusted the person that was in my bed and I instantly trusted the situation.

Haley and I were talking non-stop and I loved it. She seemed to be perfect to me and I to her. Our third night was as perfect of a night I think I'll ever have. The night started at my apartment with drinks. We put on music and just talked as we fell into further inebriation. We were in my kitchen, at my table playing music when the classic "Hard to Handle" by Otis Redding came on.

We danced in my kitchen stopping to kiss. That moment is still one my favorite memories, in general, it needs be taken out of context for me to truly enjoy it. This moment is something that still comes to my mind. The thoughts and feelings of what would transpire later, are kept at bay. I think back and don't think about the past, or the near future after this moment. Instead, I look back and I remember her beauty and the moment I realized life is shit at times, but it's these moments that I have to look forward to with whomever it may be.

We told each other we were in love with one another that night. I was on cloud nine. The rest of the night we went from club to club drinking and finding solace in alcohol. We repeated what we had just declared.

I fucked up, hard.

I thought I was truly happy. My apartment felt new again, work felt fun and most of all, I was excited about being alive in a new city. I had Haley to thank for that. I wrapped so much of myself too early on in her. While things were as perfect as I thought they could ever be, I was hiding my secret about the church.

I had not told Haley about my struggle with the church. I had to slowly bridge that gap, since I led her to believe that I was not an active member of the church is anyway, shape or form. This would happen very shortly.

Easter was approaching and I did not have plans until Haley invited me to come to easter dinner with her and her family. I hesitantly accepted. I was hesitant because what I learned from attending the super bowl party with Abigail and her Ex's family, I can be awkward and shy around significant other's family.

Easter dinner consisted of Haley's brother and his girlfriend, her mother and mother's boyfriend, then her and I. At this point, it felt more than it really was. Even though I openly and almost eagerly jumped into a relationship with her, this was beginning to feel too much for me.

Only a couple of things really stuck out. One of them was that Haleys mother's boyfriend kept making references to the church. I really did not want to talk about that subject. I felt like I was being a hypocrite. Which I was, but it was easier to just ignore it. It also had to do with the fact that Haley and I had actively been having sex, so I did not feel like I was in any place to speak about the church since I was not living a "righteous lifestyle." I felt like a piece of shit because I was still going back and forth when it came to holding myself accountable to the church's standards. It would take me several more months to realize I was not a piece of shit, just confused.

This is the logic religion can easily put into your head. If you fail to live up to certain standards, you're the problem.

After dinner, Haley and I took a walk around the neighborhood. Haley lived in the Avenues, as well. During our walk,

the church came up, which did happen often. This line of questioning was different though. She asked me all about the church and the role it had in my life.
I confessed to everything. My struggles, my wantonness to be active, my wantonness to not be a member of church and how it really all depended on the day. I spoke about my mission and how much I loved it.
The thought of truly leaving the church scared me. At times I regretted every "sin" I had committed, then at times I regretted being baptized. She then said something that surprised me.
She asked if she can come to church with me. I was almost speechless and hit with a rush of fantasies, all at once. My mind filled with thoughts of her and I walking hand in hand to the temple counting our blessings. I imagined being the "can-do" LDS couple that was edgy and cultured, yet still clung to traditional values. I imagined the perfect churchy-fairytale story.
I wasted no time in telling people at church about her coming. I wanted her first time coming to church to be perfect. The reason I told people in church was because they can help her have a great, even it's a pseudo experience.
When I was a missionary, we had meetings with ward members about how we can best bring someone unto the gospel.

Often, one of the biggest topics we discussed was "fellowshipping." Fellowshipping is a term best described as an "assigned friend." The goal of a fellowshipper is to be there for them so that they'll have a friend to rely on within the gospel. Someone independent of the missionary's. Someone to confide in and ask questions that they were maybe too embarrassed to ask out loud. I spoke with the women at the church and they were eager to "fellowship" her. The logic of a fellowshipper is wrong. An assigned friend is fake and only serves the purpose of joining the church. On my mission, I saw hardly any fellowshippers actually stay friends with the perspective member, after the baptism.

Often after the individual has been baptized, the fellowshipper falls back into the congregation and they may still talk, but the relationship is clearly different. I really did want this to be a special event, even though I knew what could happen with a fellowshipper. I wanted this to be an opportunity to be active and I once again, took this as a sign from God that I was to be active and a contributing member of the church.

Her first time at church was to be her only time and last time. It was anything, but perfect. It turned out to

be a huge stepping stone in my pathway out of the church.
I picked Haley up for church and we made our way a couple blocks down to the building. for first hour, the males and the females separate. Haley had been so excited to come to church, but the look of fear in her eyes when it came to say goodbye for that first hour, still brings small chuckles to my mind when I think about it.
I do not know how it feels for a parent to drop their child off at kindergarten for the first time, but I imagine it is similar to what I felt and how Haley looked. Her puppy dog looking face was enough for me to feel like I was even more in love with her.
During Elder's Quorum, I couldn't help but feel anxious. The reason being, I hoped that the message in Relief society was able to register with Haley. It did not.
Sunday school was not very memorable, so on to sacrament. This was a supposed to be a defining moment for Haley and the church, as well as my relationship with the church.
Saying the church is "organized religion" is an understatement. The church is so deep and intricate that it is easy to not fully grasp all of it. The church is led by the First presidency, which consists of three men and the quorum of the twelve apostles. Underneath them, are the quorums of the

seventy. There are multiple quorums. Each member of each qucrum is in charge of different departments, are on different boards and travel all over the world.

That particular sunday in church, we had a member of the second quorum of the seventy speaking at sacrament. His name was Elder Golden.

When I saw that a member of the second quorum of the seventy was to be speaking at church, I almost could not contain my excitement. I considered this a home-run. Surely he'll know what to say to make Haley believe everything that, I, myself was unsure about on a day-to-day basis. I had heard so many stories and confessions about how the simple, yet powerful words of one of the leaders of the church had "changed the most stubborn of hearts." I thought this would be one such moment.

Elder Golden began speaking on the importance faith has in one's live. The talk began great. It had great content and was very simple and easy to understand. However, it began to take a turn that I can only describe as asinine. He began to speak about atheists. He said "I want to ask them what are they smoking?" The crowd laughed at the thought of a church leader using such language in such a "sacred" setting, to them, this was funny because they thought the same logic, while they may not condone his language, they condoned his logic. I was appalled and offended. He did not stop though. He mentioned Hyde Park in London. Hyde Park is one of the largest parks in London. He mentioned he would like to "Erect a statue that says "oh thou foolishness." I was even more embarrassed and regretted inviting Haley. Elder Golden was appointed a member of the Seventy on March 31, 2001.

In May of 1983, the now deceased, Elder Boyd K. Packer who was a member of the Quorum of the twelve apostles, gave a talk to the churches coordinating council. This talk was meant for a specific audience so he is rather open with his comments. Elder Packer is speaking of the "enemies" of the church.

"The dangers I speak of come from the gay-lesbian movement, the feminist movement (both of which are relatively new), and the ever-present challenge from the so-called scholars or intellectuals. Our local leaders must deal with all three of them with ever-increasing frequency. In each case, the members who are hurting have the conviction that the Church somehow is doing something wrong to members or that the Church is not doing enough for them."

The church has since changed the way it handles the "enemies of the church." In 2015, the church pushed forward bills that push religious freedom as well as protection against discrimination for LGBT and religious groups. The separation of church and state does not exist in Utah politics.

The reason this is important is because these comments made by Elder golden came right after a critical time when the church was actively trying to change its image in regards to acceptance. These statements did not happen in front of a large group, nor was it published for millions to read. It was said on a Sunday in May and had a big enough impact to lead me to question the church and enough to convince, even Haley further, she was right. For one of the first times in my life, I was embarrassed to be LDS. I was embarrassed because I did not agree with him, yet I supported the very church he had an integral part in leading.

Was I to believe this man was speaking his personal opinion or was he just being more open about the church's stance? The line was blurred to an unrecognizable point.

The LDS church holds their semi-annual general conference in April and October. The previous month, April, was general conference. During general conference you sustain the church leaders. You agree that they are called of god to bring about his work on this earth. You raise your "arm to the square" and unanimously agree that these men are called of god. That sustaining included Elder Golden. I had sustained the man that had made the most asinine comments I had ever heard from a church member over the pulpit. After Elder Golden made those comments and the meeting was over, I wished to speak with him about his choice words. I spoke with him and how offended I was, as well as Haley. He apologized profusely. I accepted. He even offered to call Haley and apologize and put his comments into context. He never called her.

This was supposed to be a joyous moment where Haley had a faith defining experience and I realize the error of my unrepentant ways.

Neither of those happened. Haley never went back to church and my faith was never the same.

I did not have time to dwell on it though because I was going to be spending time in California with my older sister. This had been months in the planning

The plan was to see Brand New in Los Angeles then head up to San Francisco. The trip was to last a week. This was going be the first time I would see my older sister, Blair in 5 years. She had been living in Hawaii since she was 19 and I had served a mission to Phoenix and moved to Salt Lake City. Neither of us had the means to freely travel, so we had not seen each other in a very long time. This trip was widely pushed by my mom but nonetheless, I was excited.

The day came when I was to fly out to Los Angeles. Things were going well between Haley and I, so well, in fact I trusted her with my apartment and my car while I was gone.

This trip was awful. Every part of it was bad. As much as I loved my older sister, I missed Haley and constantly talking to her was not helping the trip go any easier. I arrived in L.A and took a shuttle to a friend of my mom's house where we would be staying while in L.A. My older sister would not arrive in Los Angeles until the following day.

I was happy to see my sister, but we were two completely different people. As mentioned before, my family was not very close growing up. I have a hard time truly being myself around my family, and that continues to this day. I just feel awkward speaking the way I want to and being who I really am around them. I cannot explain it.

This trip was no exception. My older sister was not making it any easier, either. She was rude and when I would make comments that were little pieces of me being myself, I was shot down. This led me to recluse even more. I couldn't wait to get to the concert

because it meant I was going to be able to finally let loose.
Brand new put on a great show. The opener was Desaparecidos, which is Conor oberst's emo/Political band. Also, built to spill played. It felt great to be able to be myself. My sister and I separated fairly early on. I love her to death, but as many should be able to relate, it was great to be away from family.
What made it so bad was the fact that it had been so long. We were both completely different people and it was easier to create tension and reasons to be mad than it was to actually talk like siblings.
I had tried to really be open at times during the course of this trip, but my older sister would not give. She was rude, impatient and did not seem to relish in the fact we were together after five years.
After L.A, we drove up to San Francisco. For those who may not know, that drive is about 6 hours. It is long and excruciatingly boring. The course of the drive was about as long as it took for me to regret this trip. This was not even the worst of it. My music was not an option. We really only agreed on two bands/artists: Brand new and David Bowie.
After time took too long to pass, we finally made it to our hotel in San Francisco. Blair had something in San

Francisco that I did not- Friends. I can pretty easily say, I definitely took a backseat to them on this trip. She knew it, I knew it and her friends very possibly knew it. I hated it. Although my plane back to Salt Lake City was already booked, I asked my mom if she was willing to pay to transfer my ticket. Nothing came of that question. I was stuck. The next day we met up with her friends and the boy she was seeing. They had previously met in Hawaii. He was from Santa Cruz. While I had nothing against him, he was part of the problem.

The next day I woke up eager to explore the city. I woke up early, went for a walk, grabbed breakfast and went back to the hotel, excited to do some exploring.

I decided to put everything that had happened behind me and try to enjoy what was left of this trip. Blair already had plans for the both of us. I went with it, thinking maybe she had the same or similar mindset. I was wrong. Her, her friends and I ended up at a bar called Zeitgeist. From what I was told, this particular bar is famous for its Bloody Marys.

We were at Zeitgeist for five hours. My frustration grew and grew to the point I could not handle it anymore. The company was great, but I did not want to spend my time in a dingy bar. (sorry Zeitgeist.) I wanted to walk on the golden gate bridge, explore Haight-Ashbury and go to Alcatraz. Not a single one of these things would happen. Part of me wanted to say "fuck it." I should have just done my own thing while there but I did not want to completely give up. I held out hope something would happen. Blair didn't want me to go out by myself, so I was stuck.

Something did happen. My Mom bought us tickets to a giants game. I was excited to go to my first baseball game. This was the season coming off their world series title. I was not prepared for the game. Goddamn, it was cold. The Giants were playing the Arizona Diamondbacks.

They were absolutely destroyed. I thought to myself "how often am I going to a game at Giant stadium?" Needless to say, I've never been back, Also, I don't care for baseball anymore than I did that night.

After the game, the plan was to go out to the mission district. I was up for it. Finally we would see part of the city. The plan was to get inebriated as fast as possible. That was the way I dealt with the way the trip had been. We took an Uber to a hotel Blairs friends were staying at. While there I sheepishly sat in the corner not saying a word. Blair had given up and so had I. Now we were just stuck together, no longer enjoying each others company.

Blair's friend had mentioned we may do cocaine. This excited me because I had done cocaine before and really enjoyed it. It would also serve as a way to escape the tension between my sister and I.

I mentioned this to Haley. Haley basically had minute to minute updates about how my trip was going. Haley was not happy with my wanting to do cocaine. In her own words she said "I don't like this, I feel like I don't know you." In hindsight, she was right. We had only been together for no more than three-four weeks, at that time. I confided in Haley and now I had nowhere to turn.

I could not speak to my sister since she was the problem and I could not talk to Haley because she was upset with me. I was stuck. I was pissed. I was pissed at my sister for not helping to make this trip what it could have been. Granted, I was to blame, as well. I was pissed at the situation and I was pissed at Haley. She had been my outlet during this whole trip and I was open with her and it backfired and pushed me into isolation.

I settled when one of the guys in attendance broke out dabs. For those unfamiliar with "dabs" it is essentially Hash oil that is burned and inhaled, generally with a bong. I've always enjoyed Dabs and had a good time whenever I did smoke it. I did them

every so often and liked it that way, at least for me, it turned me into a vegetative state. So I decided to get as high as possible.
This was the highest I have ever been. My body started to go numb within ten minutes, which is also how long it took me to stop coughing. I decided to stay in that night. I was so damn upset. Finally we were gonna be going out, but I got way too high to function. This was just another small step that leads me to the conclusion that my life never works out how I want it to.
Blair did not seem to upset by this. I let the high take over and at some point I drifted off to sleep.
Haley and I eventually made up and I was on my way to the airport to head back to Salt Lake City. All the fighting her and I had done seemed so miniscule and petty because I was about to see her. Within myself, I tried to downplay how excited I was. I wanted to act like the scene out of a movie was a regular occurrence. It was not. I just pretended it was.
I landed at Salt Lake international eager to grab my bag and be reunited with Haley. Movies make this moment seem so perfect in every which way and it is. Hugging Haley felt so right and I did not want that moment to end. We walked out to my jeep and we drove back to my apartment.

On the drive back, I asked Haley if she had been to my apartment and she told me no. Haley and I arrived at my apartment, hand in hand. She had cleaned my apartment, bought me groceries and even brought some clothes over to keep for overnight stays. I was so flattered by this and I felt so undeserving of her. Never in my life had anyone done this for me. She wanted to be with me and I truly realized it at that point. She was in it for the long haul and I realized it at that point. She loved me for me. Or so I thought. I had never even considered lust as an option. I had never considered this would end, so why would I then?

Things were about to change and I had not the slightest clue.

Haley and I had completely different schedules. I worked 9-5, she generally worked 4-11. I tried not to let this get in the way.

Often times, I would walk to her work and walk her back to my place, or give her a ride home. This was not sustainable, though. A friend once said "if you have opposite schedules it's just not gonna work." I told them they were dumb and had no idea what they were talking about. They were correct. I was the one that was dumb and had no idea what I was talking about.

On April 29, 2015 my beloved Trail Blazers were playing a must win game

against the Memphis Grizzlies in the western conference playoffs. This night I was up late for several reasons.
The first being for work. The owner of the property I worked at was having one of his assistants come out and oversee his Utah properties. His name was Travis. He was driving from San Diego. He was not expected to arrive until about 10:30-11PM. I was to be the one to show him around the property and give him keys and such. Whenever tedious errands and little chores had to be done at work, it was me that was assigned the task. This was also about the time Haley was hopefully going to be getting off.
The second was the blazer game. I needed to see if my team could prevail. I went to Haley's work that night to watch the game, await for her to get off work and leave at some point to let Travis into his new home.
The Blazers were in a close game, but Memphis was being led by former Trailblazer, Zach Randolph. As the night wore on, so did Haley's shift and the Blazers hope of winning. I eventually had to leave to tend to work. When I had been told a few days earlier that I was going to be helping Travis move in, my first impressions was that this guy was an old fat cat in the real estate business. I could not have been more wrong.

Travis is only a few years older than me and is an awesome guy. One of the last things we talked about, was the apartment complex and all the details of that. Instead we talked about sports, school and life. He is an awesome guy. I ran into Travis probably 3 months later, at a bar. We drank and talked like old friends.

After I had taken care of work, I drove back to Whiskey Street to await the end of Haley's shift. My Blazers lost. 93-99. Dammit. Haley eventually got off work and joined me at the bar. I was so tired, I had already worked all day and had been up way past my bedtime.

Haley wanted to unwind after work, with a beer and I was fine with that. I, however, made a big mistake that at the time, I did not realize the magnification of what I asked. If I had not asked that question would this chapter not exist? Would her and I still be together? Possibly married? The question and possible outcomes are numerous and I cannot fathom all of them, but I can't help but feel that if I had kept my mouth shut, things would have been different?

Haley finished her first beer. I thought that would be the end. She ordered a second one. So I asked her "Do you think you'll be done with that soon?" Holy shit, I get the dirtiest look I had ever seen her give. She looked at me like I had just said the most vile and disgusting thing to ever have been uttered.

Her mood instantly changed and her demeanor reflected that. She became really irritated and accused me of trying to rush her. She finished her beer in a bad mood and we arrived at my car and what ensued, altered our relationship to a state that was not repairable.

Our argument was not about what had just happened. That was a small fraction of it. She spoke of problems we had that I had been reluctant to address because I wanted to suppress them.

After probably 10 minutes of going back and forth, I decided it was not worth it. This was our first true fight. I was irate, she was irate. She kept bringing up new topics before I could even dispel the previous one. Whether I was or not, I felt I was being attacked. I began to think about just getting out of the situation.

No true resolve, just a way out. If I had any chance of this relationship lasting, it was to apologize and end it. So that is what I did. She accepted it and we went back to my apartment and went to bed.

The next day, something was off. I could not put my finger on it, but I texted Haley and she did not respond. I did not think much of it. The next day after was my day off. Haley worked at night so it was perfect We were gonna spend the day together until she had to go into work.

I picked her up and we went to lunch. This was to be our last meal, together. Awkward conversation and quietness ruled the meal. After lunch, Haley had the idea to go to a nearby park and go for a walk. While I had noticed lunch was off compared to what we were used to, I did not suspect the next transpiring events.

Haley, before had mentioned that she needed to know I cared for her and thought she was beautiful. This went without saying, easily. I do not believe I ever neglected this, but I brought this up in the fact that, I, too needed the same reassurance she was always asking for and wanting. I, too wanted to be told the same things. That she loved me, that she cared for me. I felt that she did, but I was just wanting the same affection.

After I began to talk about the wantonness of this she said "lets go over here I need to talk to you." That was when I realized why she had not texted me back or reassured me of anything. She didn't feel that way anymore. Just as quickly as we had fallen head over heels in love, she was retracing her steps and reversing every feeling she had had for me.

Haley used an excuse. Rather than be direct, she said "You need to find out if you're going to be active in the church. I do not want anything to do with the church." She also snuck in "plus I want to be single." I was devastated.

I drove her home and we had one last kiss. I went into a deep thought. I did not acknowledge the latter statement. I did not want to. My thought process was "Leave the church, and you have the girl. Stay active and she is gone." I did not want to acknowledge the latter statement because of the fears I ignored the first night we met, were beginning to enter the picture. The fear of my inner self telling me "I told you so" was not something I wanted to hear. How the fuck could I have been so stupid as to ignore, myself and my friends? I know this happens all the time, but damn. I fucked up hard this time.

I went through a mental breakdown that I have yet to have since. I was torn. A life of blessings and bliss, or a life with the woman I love?

I had a hard time abandoning what I knew, yet I was already on the cusp of leaving the church so would it be bad if I took just one step further? Was I guaranteed a life with Haley if I do leave?

I decided to leave the church. Not because I had thought it all the way through, but because I decided Haley was more important. I made this decision not because I thought the church through and decided I did not believe the doctrine. While I didn't fully believe, I decided to leave and not practice what I did believe. I felt I could hide that desire for a lifetime and be the person Haley wanted me to be.

Once my decision was made, I texted Haley and said I had "made my decision. I'm all yours, Babe!" (How fucking cringey.)I really felt that all I had to do. Though, she was not sincere in giving me that ultimatum. If she had been, shouldn't she have given me the benefit of the doubt? Shouldn't she have been happy for me? Embraced me? None of these were what I was to experience. Our relationship was over. I felt so embarrassed. I felt embarrassed that I could not be the person Haley confided in. I could not be the person Haley dumped all her toils and cares from the day on. I was not going to be the person Haley looked forward to seeing. Instead I was hung out to dry and forgotten about.

I even showed up at her work to tell her the news, to no avail.

Mine and Haley's past relationship was just that. In the past.

What embarrassed me the most was how open and candid and I had been with Haley right before we broke up. I opened up and told her about my insecurities and need to be reassured.

What the fuck. I opened up and had my insecurities stomped on and thrown around. I felt so embarrassed and ashamed.

As much of a cliche as it may sound, it is reasons like this being open and honest scares so many people. The thought that someone can be your best friend and confidant, then the next day, or in this case the very same day, be a complete stranger is a scary thought.

I sank into a deep depression. My lowest point was when it came to throwing her stuff away. Haley had left various clothes at my apartment. When I took her clothes out of my dresser, I sobbed for a solid ten minutes. I was a mess. I could not wrap my head around us not being together. I did not want to move on. I wanted to go back to the way things were before. I constantly thought "Why wasn't I good enough?" "What could I have done differently?"

These thoughts are poisonous. They do nothing but break you down even more than you already are. Just because things do not work out it is not because something was lacking. It is because compatibility did not work in the end.

Trying to put a square peg into a round hole does not have to do with anything lacking, it has to do with compatibility. There is nothing wrong with either party they just do not fit together. I did not realize this until months later.

Despite all this, I was still falling at her feet whether she knew it or not. About a month later, I texted Haley and asked to grab drinks with the perception that I was over it and I more so just wanted to catch up and see how she was doing. That was about as far from the truth as can be. I was still crazy over her and in love even more than the day I first told her. As I was sitting on the porch of the Copper Common nervously drinking my rum and coke. I saw her walk up. Oh my goodness, she was just as beautiful as I remember. She was wearing an olive-green dress that flowed as the wind blew. She came out and I acted surprised to see her.

We spoke effortlessly. Our conversation flowed and it felt like old times. I tried to gauge the situation by looking into her eyes. As cheesy and Nicholas Sparks as that sounds, I firmly believe that if you can look a girl in the eye and she does not look away after about 2 seconds there is some sort of connection. She looked away almost every-time. I knew she didn't feel any connection anymore, but I pressed on. I continued to slip further and further into inebriation. As I did, I felt the urge to bring up our past. Though I did fight this urge as long as I was able to. I then suggested we leave and go for a walk. She obliged and we left. We were walking west on 300 South when we turned right onto State street. I stopped and said "Haley, I'm still in love with you." I had envisioned this moment many times in the head.

The outcome I was wanting and wishing for, was that she realized that it was a mistake that we were not together and she would confess her love for me and we would kiss and hug.

All the troubles would be gone and life would be magical. That did not happen. The reality was that I was drunkenly confessing my love for her and asking to get back together.

She insisted that we not get back together. She went on to tell me one of the most fucked up things you can ever tell someone in this situation.

She told me about a guy she had been seeing and how she wanted to date him so bad and she had been in my situation about a week earlier. What the fuck? Why would you tell me that? How the hell do you think that is a beneficial to the current situation? It is not. I am convinced she told me that to intentionally hurt me. It worked, not at the time, but eventually in later reflections of this event. Haley went her way and I went mine.

I, still to this day, do not understand why she told me this. I think her goal was to form a connection that she knew what I was going through. Not only did she not make a connection, she made me feel awful about myself.

Once again, I opened up to her and once again I felt embarrassed. Even after that, I still tried to convince her. I learned if you need to convince someone to like you, stop. You're just embarrassing yourself even more.

I was drunk and an emotional mess on the corner of 300 S and State. I called my mom. I never talk to family about relationship or really about life in general. I am a very reserved person. I spoke with my mom for about 10 minutes. I cannot remember the conversation we had. I remember sitting on the steps of an office building with my phone in my hand and not giving a care about who saw me cry. I didn't know these people, why should I care?

Haley and I would eventually grab coffee several times in the months following, but nothing came out of it. I moved on and she ended up in another relationship. I have mixed emotions about our time together as well as the fallout.

When I made the decision to leave the church for Haley, that decision stuck, for the most part. I would end up going to church a couple more times before I fully left. It is hard to say if my life is better now that I left the church but I also do not know if my life would be better if I was still active in the church. However, I am a much happier person.

It was 100 percent completely wrong for her to give me that ultimatum. It was wrong of her to lead me on when I was nothing more than a rebound. I should have seen that I was just that. I was blind, lonely and in denial. I decided to give into a situation I should not have been in. However, by that same token, it was wrong for me to lie about such a deep and divisive theme in my life.

From what I'm aware of, Haley is now in a relationship that started several months after her and I broke up. I hope she is happy, I really do. However, I still to this day hold anger. I did not deserve to be treated that way. if I saw her on the street and the past came up, I would not hesitate to tell her how terrible it was what she put me through.

I made many mistakes in this situation. I mistook lust for love. In a very short time, I had such a wide range of emotions, it was hard to even know what I wanted. I did not know what I wanted for the future. To be a member? Forsake the church? Though, I was mad at Haley, I did not give her an ideal situation, just as she hadn't given me one. It was just a shitty situation for all parties involved.

Beginning of Summer, 2015
Chapter 6

The beginning of my first summer in Salt Lake City was not how I had imagined it would be. I was reeling from a recent break up that took everything out of me. I would wake up with no motivation for work. I went home with eve less motivation to work on my passions of playing music and writing. I would just eat a shitty meal and go to bed with no real goals or aspirations.

As time went on, I became determined to change this mindset. I didn't want to just exist, I wanted to truly live. I wanted to make the most of this move. Sitting home and crying "Woe is me" was not working for me. I was done wallowing in self-pity.

One of my best friends, Justen and a couple of our mutual friends were on a trip across the west. They were road tripping to random camping spots, national parks and just overall, doing exactly what I wanted to do. I had first learned about this months in advance. Haley and I had planned on meeting them down in southern Utah. Haley and I wanted to explore, camp and hike together. Her and I planned on taking this trip together.

The plans were set in stone, she had even requested time off from work for this trip. The camping trip was planned for about a month after Haley and I had broken up. That just proved to me that the break up was a sudden and swift declaration she had made.

It was almost as if she woke up on day and had a sudden change of heart. The feelings and the "I love you's" were no longer seen as something sustainable and tangible. She saw them as they were. A hindrance.

After Haley and I broke up, our pictures were deleted off of Instagram, she separated completely. This did nothing but destroy me, further.

Justen and our mutual friends were aware of this. They knew I was not okay. They knew my mental state of being was fragile, at best. They knew I was having a tough moment in my life. Had I realized it was lust, not love, I would have been fine. Nevertheless, I still planned on getting together with them. I needed this trip. My mind needed this trip.

As the time approached for them to come, the plan was they would get a hotel room in Salt Lake City and stay for the night. I would then meet them at the hotel and we would go from there.

I awaited the call from Justen saying that they had arrived at their hotel. I sat in my apartment stewing and waiting. My chest began to pound because I was excited to have a sense of normalcy in my life. I wanted them to see my apartment. Though, I may not have been doing good, I hung my head on the fact I had my own apartment. As weird as that may sound, I was proud of that and I wanted others to relish in it with me.

I got the phone call and I basically ran to my Jeep. It was a rainy, but warm night. I was sweating in my multiple layers while I put my car in drive and left as fast as I could.

They were staying at a hotel out by the Salt Lake City airport. Growing up in Portland, the PDX airport was always seen a far destination and growing up without a lot of money, was hardly ever a destination we went to.

The Salt Lake Airport is very different. It's closer and easier to

navigate. It's mostly known for the extravagant celebrations that take place when a returned missionary returns home.
Words cannot describe the frustration when it comes to trying to navigate that airport. Most of the time, there is nothing but a lake of blonde-hair, blue-eyed Mormons celebrating a loved one coming home from their mission. Balloons, signs and yells all become clearly evident.
As I headed west for the airport, I didn't listen to music. I was too preoccupied by the thought of seeing friends, for the first time in months. I arrived and was happy to be greeted by Justen.
We shared a hug and we entered the room where our other friends were. I gave our friend Chad a hug and shook hands with two other acquaintances. The biggest point of discussion they had, was how their order at In n' out was wrong and they wanted to take this up with the restaurant. That particular restaurant was 15 minutes north of Salt Lake City in a town called Farmington. There is not one in downtown proper. Which, if you want a business venture, open one in downtown Salt Lake City, and you'll never worry about money

again. Their journey north was not to be happening tonight.
The plan was to drive back into Salt Lake City and check out the city. This was a Sunday night. In most cities, though, work is the next day, there is still a prevalent nightlife. Not in Salt Lake City. Sundays turn the city into a ghost-town.
Even the city's largest mall, City Creek, is shut down because it's church owned. Most people stay away, except for the tourists who definitely end up disappointed.
Bars are still open, but their attendance is not nearly as much as it is on a Saturday night. This night was no exception.
We arrived at my apartment. We were there for about 10 minutes before we decided on a plan. The plan was to grab food at the Pie hole, then we would head out to the bars.
Salt Lake City is not very walkable. 1 city block in Salt Lake City is comparable to roughly 6 Portland blocks. The city is hilly and crosswalks are few and far in between. This was something Justen and Chad discovered as we were walking.
In reality, the pizza shop was 5 blocks away, but the exchange rate

made it roughly 30 Portland blocks. Their patience for the amount of walking was not there that night. We decided to go to a nearby bar, instead.

While there, a comment was made about how deserted it was. That was when I spoke about this city on Sundays. "It's not a very culturally exciting spot. You more-so take what you can get in this city."

The night was not very exciting. Mostly drinks, fries from beer bar and conversation. The next day we would be heading south for Goblin Valley. The trip that Haley was supposed to be accompanying me on.

The next morning came, and it was time for me to head back out to the hotel they were staying at. Justen and I were going to drive to southern Utah, just us two. The others were going to be in their car.

As I picked up Justen, a sense of normalcy began to set in. Driving with a true friend is not something I had not done in a long time. Driving with friends, listening to music and just talking, is something I had done 100 times over in my life.

This time was different, though. This time was much needed and wanted. We drove down to southern Utah and made stops along the way to take pictures. Photography is something that Justen is passionate about. For me, it more of a hobby. We drove the windy roads through the national parks and made our way to the campground. Goblin Valley looks like it is something meant to be on Mars, it's outer worldly.

As we pulled into our campsite, the consensus was, let's set up after doing some hiking. Goblin Valley does not have many trail's, rather, you just kind of walk and explore. As I walked the grounds, traversed caves and climbed rocks, I couldn't help but think about the companion I was supposed to have.

Was she thinking about me? Was she missing me? I didn't have cell phone service for that day and I had hoped that when I would get service, I may have a missed call, text or even voicemail from her. I was hoping for a text that may have contained everything from "let's grab a drink?" to "I've been thinking about you."

None of this happened, and why should it? Instead, I tried my best to concentrate on my friends and forget about her because she had clearly forgotten about me. She didn't care about me at that point. She was already dating other people and probably falling in love with them.

As the day wore on and the sky shifted to the evening, it was time to head back to camp. As we began walking back, it became noticeably cooler. When that happens, the desert animals begin to come out. As we were walking we could see a snake that was probably four feet long, up against the rocks. We noped the fuck out because we didn't know the type of snake it was, so it was easier just to be smart about it. When we got to camp, everyone began setting up their tents. I didn't have a tent because I had a different plan.

I still had my Jeep, and planned on sleeping in the back. The reason I bought a car as big as my jeep, was for this exact reason. I didn't want to be held back by my car.

Our campground was situated at the foot of a rock wall. This rock wall had a column sticking out and between the rock and the wall, sat a perfectly formed seat. I sat there while everyone was setting up their tents and getting situated.

I took this time to think about the future.

Here I was, camping while my life seemed to be in a rut. As I looked out over the valley and saw the places I had just been, all the rocks and cliffs I had climbed and traversed, I couldn't help but notice, I was looking down on them. Hiking had been hard and not something I was prepared for, but with the help of my friends, I was able to overcome those difficulties and continue on. Granted, there were times I was tired and sore, but here I was overlooking the trials I had just faced.

I was going to be ok. In the meantime though, it was all about how I dealt with it. Sure there was going to be better days than some, but those bad days are what make the good days worth it.

As my friends finished setting up their campsites, I eventually descended and joined them. It was time for dinner. They were all very experienced campers so naturally we had the meat, veggies, beer and weed.

We cooked our dinner, played some guitar, and caught up while in front of the fire. Next to our campsite was an opening into a small valley with no campsites. That was to be the spot we would smoke. We gathered our weed and pipe and embarked about 50 yards to the right of the campsite.

By the time we finished smoking, it was time for bed. I had to wake up early the next morning because I had to get home for work in the coming days. I was only going to be on this leg of the trip.

I put my backseat down, climbed into the back of my Jeep and laid down while wrapped up in my sleeping bag. I was high and listening to the album Lonerism by Tame Impala. For the first time in two months I was not thinking about Haley. I was thinking about how high I was. It had been a while.

While it may have been my current state of inebriation, it was something to distract me from what my constant thought had been. My two constant thoughts were as followed:
-How in "love" I am with Haley.
-How much I miss Haley.

I awoke early the next morning, which is something I do now and have always done. I've always been a morning person. I awoke sore and ready to leave.

I had had a moment of clarity the evening before while sitting atop a rock. It was time to put that moment to the test.

I got out of my jeep, walked over to Justen's tent and said goodbye. I would be seeing him again very soon. I drove back to Salt Lake City, truly seeing the beauty of the state. I saw the red rock of the desert, the rolling, green hills and the charming small towns.

I arrived back at my apartment, showered and slept. The rest of the day was not very memorable.

That Jeep would eventually die, as well. It died while in Little Cottonwood canyon, which lies about 20 minutes southeast of Salt Lake City. To this day, still one of my favorite cars I've ever owned.

I continued working and merely just existing. While my overall mood began to change, I still wasn't having the best experience I wanted to get out of this move.

I had completely stopped going to church. It happened sooner than I thought it would. While Haley had pushed me to a decision, I still had my reservations about leaving. I went to church probably another 3 weeks after Haley and I had broken up.

One sunday I was asked to teach a lesson in Elders Quorum. I agreed. I believe I was asked because they saw me slipping. They saw that I was close to leaving. In the church when that happens, members believe giving the person in question a task is a good way to bring them back. They believe that the person struggling, if asked to help others, will be rejuvenated in their belief system and activity within the church. This was not the case for me.

I taught Elders Quorum and as I spoke all the routine things such as "Jesus loves you," "Blessings are yours for the taking" and "I know the church is true," It did not sound right to me anymore. It did not sound familiar, it did not ring true anymore. It sounded foreign and unwanted.

I went about the rest of my meetings by myself. Sitting in the back and keeping to myself. Once again, nothing that day sounded true, right, or brought about the "warmth" of the spirit.

What really made me shy away was the social aspect of church and how non-existent that was for me. I made a proclamation. I decided I was not going to go to church for however long it took for people to notice I was missing.

This was a definitely a spiritual russian roulette. This was a "risk" I was willing to take. Truth is, I had no intention of going back. My mind had been made up before I even realized it had been made for me, by me. I just needed a half-hearted effort to justify it.

After a month, I received a phone call. The phone call was from a member of the church. He asked if him and a member of the ward leadership could come over and sit down with me. I agreed. I have no problem having people from the church over, as a missionary, I learned to at least hear people out. They came over one evening and we spoke. They were at my apartment for about an hour.

During this hour, we discussed all about my concerns. I didn't have just social concerns, at this point. I had doctrinal concerns, as well. I had questions about the history of the church and about the character of Joseph Smith. None of my questions were able to be answered. Instead, I got the same answers I fed people on my mission.

"You just have to have faith," "We don't know why the lord asked that of him." As a missionary, I gave these answers to people all the time. I was always in a stupor of thought that these answers did not suffice.

While being on the opposing end of these answers, I realized how frustrating it was to hear those answers. I realized, it did not progress my thoughts and beliefs. It just angered me that my question could not be answered.

I never went to church again. It's a little eerie that the last time I went to church, was the last time I taught other members about the gospel.

Leaving the church was not nearly as climactic as I thought it would be. Instead, it came as a no-brainer.

As time went on, I began going out with Rob. The rob from my first job in South Jordan, not from the Covey. Though, I would eventually go out with both.

Rob from South Jordan and I became really good friends. This particular night, we went out looking to talk to people and meet new friends. Rob came over to my apartment for some drinks and conversation. It had been a minute since we got together.

As Rob and I caught up I finally began to feel that Haley was behind me. I would have several other run ins with her over the next couple years, but without the emotions of our relationships past.

Rob and I walked the 3 blocks to Beer Bar and bought our drinks. It was a friday night and the bar was packed. As mentioned before, Beer Bar is one, if not the most popular bar in Salt Lake City. This was the reason we had trouble finding seating. We eventually found seating at one of the many rows of tables. We sat across from a couple we have never seen before. Their names were Allyssa and Ryan.

Allyssa and Ryan appeared to not be from around here. They appeared to be there by themselves, while drinking their drinks, they seemed a bit reserved.

Rob and I made small talk with the both of them. They were from Kentucky and had moved to Salt Lake City because Allyssa's work had asked her to move. By the end of our 15-20 minute conversation, I found out, this couple I had never met, had my phone number in Ryan's phone. "Aaron SLC" was what my contact name was in his phone. How is that even possible? Not even an hour before, we had no idea each other existed. Well, we have to go back several months to February, 2015. It was around this time that Allysaa and Ryan knew that they would be moving.

They began to shop for some apartments in the Salt Lake area. One of the apartments they looked at was an apartment at the Covey. Since they were in Kentucky at the time, we would have to FaceTime. This is how they ended up with my number. The FaceTime itself wasn't very memorable. I mostly just said comments such as, "And here is the kitchen.." also, "and there is your bathroom." It was about 10 minutes and I forgot all about it.

Before we made this connection, however, we had been making small talk. Ryan asked what we do for work. We both answered "property management." As I began explaining where I worked, Allyssa interrupted me and shouted "DO YOU WORK AT THE COVEY?" Wide-eyed and surprised, I answered "yes." That is when Ryan pulled out his phone and showed me "Aaron SLC."

For the longest time, Ryan's name in my phone was "Ryan Kentucky" and Allyssa was "Allyssa Kentucky." That night, I met two people that would turn out to be two of the most important people I met while living in Salt Lake City.

That night the liquor poured while we talked and talked. Us four eventually left and sought out food.

Rather than go to pie hole, we found a pizza shop, that would take almost another year before we realized where it was and what it was called. We were too inebriated to take mental notes.

We then parted ways. Rob and I walked back to my apartment, Allyssa and Ryan drove to theirs. The night was over, but a crucial friendship was just beginning.

Mid-summer, 2015
Chapter 7

Allyssa and Ryan had only lived in Utah for about 3 months before we had met. We continued to hangout and talk. Meeting a new friend in your early twenties is interesting. It's weird because you find yourself thinking about someone else, but not in a romantic sense. It really throws you through a loop for a minute.

Oddly enough, before I would eventually leave Salt Lake City, Rob would never hang out with Allyssa, Ryan or I at once, again. Mine and Rob's friendship wavered. We would go months before getting together, or even talking. Because of this, Allyssa, Ryan and I became very close.

We became so close in fact, we spent our 4th of July together. I didn't have any previous plans, neither did they, so why not?

The plan was to grab pizza before the festivities started. We agreed on Pie hole (of course) but we ended up going somewhere else that escapes my memory.

The plan was to begin drinking at Allyssa and Ryan's place before hiking the living room hike, which lies up behind the university of Utah campus. Since my jeep had died, I was picked up and we headed back to their place. When we arrived we began drinking and played Creedence Clearwater revival. This was about as cliche as it can get. All that was missing was a banner that said "Murica." I didn't care though. I was just happy to be with friends. As awkward conversations began, Ryan suggested we go throw a football around. I agreed, because it had been years since I had done that. We walked the three levels down to the apartment complex's pool. To the right of the pool was a patch of grass where we would be throwing the football around.

We talked, drank and overall just had a good time. I finally began to feel like Salt Lake was the city for me. I was making friends away from the church and having a hell of a good time doing so.

Now that I had left the church, it was time for a fresh start and this was it. I was about to be null and void of the church for the first time since I was 17. (I was 23 at this time.)

As time progressed, it was eventually time for us to head to the hike.

We grabbed our camping chairs and went. We drove up to the University of Utah campus and began hiking. None of us had done the hike before and it showed.

Allyssa was wearing flip-flops, which is never a good idea. As we tried to keep moving forward, we realized it was time to give up. We were not prepared for this hike, at all.

defeated and tired, we walked back down. We found a patch of elephant grass just off the trail. We set up our chairs and continued drinking. Here we were, just three friends watching fireworks. If this moment represented a new start, I was okay with that. I had three friends in all of Utah and I knew that was good enough for me. As you'll read, Allyssa and Ryan helped me out a lot. They were just all-around great people who entered my life exactly when I needed them. I do not believe in god, but I think there was some sort of divine intervention when it came to meeting them, whatever/whoever that divine being may be, thank you.

I mentioned that I would be seeing Justen again very soon. I had planned on going back to Portland for Blair's wedding.

My best friend, the man who baptized me, had met the girl he was made for. I was not going to miss that for the world. I began planning my trip. However, I had work to deal with.

As time went on, I was still working at the Covey. Cricket was long gone, work was no longer fun anymore. I thrive best in an environment where my coworkers are like family. We had that at the Covey for a while, but it began to fall apart.

Spencer, the regional manager began to ask certain questions to our property manager. These questions were way more inappropriate than any single person should ask, let alone someone in his position.

Spencer began to wonder If Rob (the maintenance tech at the Covey)and Jourdan, the assistant property manager, were having an affair. What the fuck? What does this have to do with work? I'm not very well versed in human resources policy, but I would assume that there may be a rule against this type of assumption.

I remember the property manager asking me if I knew anything regarding this. I was not as straightforward with my answer as I should have been. The truth is, I should have said no, and that she should not be asking me those types of questions. I replied "I have no Idea." She said "Ok" and I thought that was the end of it.

I called both Rob and Jourdan to let them know that people were asking questions. I did what any friend would do and I called both of them. As time would go on, this subject would come up every so often. Despite this, I began to have a renewed sense of purpose at work. I was finally clicking on all cylinders and things began to make sense. I began to not just perform, but succeed at my job.

Until one day, Spencer was on the property, which was nothing new. Spencer was on property about once a week.

At work, our clock-in system was done completely online. This day, mine did not work. I could not log-in. I just figured the computer system was down, because that had happened company-wide recently. This was also the day I was leaving for Portland. I was leaving work early that day and had everything planned out.

Rob, the Rob from South Jordan, was going to cover for me for the afternoon. I worked on various files, answered emails, took phone calls and worked hard. Rob came to the office and I let him know how the rest of his day would go. I spoke to him about the appointments, the paperwork, I showed him around the property and I even told him how I felt I was ready to advance in my career with Alliance.

Rob and I came back to the office. We said our goodbyes and he went to grab lunch, then would come back and I would leave.

As Rob left, my property manager called me into her office. I had been written up before for problems that at the time, if had I had a backbone, I could have had them dismissed. Not this time.

Spencer sat in the far chair, while I sat in the open chair. I was expecting some sort of discipline because I had yet to finish my training, which had been brought up several times before. Whatever, I'll just bite my tongue and call it good.

"Aaron, We have to let you go." I could have choked on my tongue. I was speechless. I could not believe it. I had been doing so well at my job and life, in general. I was finally growing into the person I wanted to become.

My property manager, whom I do not wish to name, mentioned our conversation regarding Rob and Jourdan having an affair. She stated "...and you told Jordan and Rob I asked about the affair. I can't trust you." This angered me to no end. How fucking dare you? That was a situation I should have never been dragged in.

When it was all said and done, they asked me if I had anything to say. I told them they were wrong to ever have asked me that question. I was pissed. I wanted to get up and flip the desk, kick the chair and scream. None of these things happened.

"It doesn't matter what I say, so I'm leaving" were my last words. I stormed out of the office in a state of disbelief. I have been given my last check and I instinctively began walking toward the bank. I called Jourdan and both Rob's and told them, but there was nothing anyone can do.

In my fury of leaving the office, I realized I had a bevy of items still at my desk. This included a jacket, speakers and other smaller miscellaneous items. I had turned my keys in, so I did not have a key. I awkwardly had to walk in and grab my stuff.

I had left jobs before, but I had never been fired. This hurt. It really did. I considered cancelling my trip to Portland to not only save money, but to wallow in my sorrows. I called my mom whom I had planned on surprising while on this trip. Surprising my mom would have shown that I was independent and able to stand on my own two feet. Calling my mom to tell her I had lost my job did the exact opposite I felt frail and weak. I was embarrassed.

My mom convinced me to go come to Portland.

The plan was to take a Craigslist rideshare, which I had found the day before. I got fired at noon, my ride was scheduled to pick me up from my apartment at three. I had everything planned, then this happened.

As I sat there in my apartment going through a myriad of emotions, I began to forget about being fired. Shit happens. I was about to go back to Portland and see my friends and family. I couldn't complain. This was going to be my time to reset, then address these issues when I got back.

I walked downstairs, bag in hand and ready to drive to Portland. The driver's name was Cassie. She got out of her car and greeted me. She asked If I could drive to begin the our trip. I obliged.

As we drove north for the Idaho border and eventually Oregon, we began our small talk. Cassie was running away. Form your own opinion, but Cassie was/is a hell of person. She was leaving her partner and her five kids. She had just quit her job and going to live with family in Oregon.

I should explain, when I said leave, it was meant to be for a only short time. Cassie was gay and her partner was nearly double her age. She was helping raise her partner's children from a previous marriage. Her separation was not meant to be permanent.

The bond Cassie and I formed over the course of this 16 hour drive is the type of bond that is formed over years of friendship. I attribute this to one big reason.

After the drive we would be going our separate ways and back to our lives. I would go on to my friend's wedding and she would go back with her family.

However, we still had this drive together. Cassie told me all about her relationship. What she loved, what she hated what she missed and wanted to change.

I told her about how I had just been fired, had just left the church and was struggling with who I was going to be as a person. We had a sense of a mutual understanding. Yes, we were at completely different spots in our lives, but we meant halfway somewhere between Salt Lake City and Portland.

The drive was abnormally long because of the Wildfires. Until the Columbia river gorge fire of 2017, Oregon was being ravaged by their worst fire season on record. Because of this, I-84 north was shut down. Instead of going north at Ontario, we would instead have to go directly west then cut up north at Salem, Oregon.

During the drive, I don't think there was one thing Cassie didn't find out out about me. I mentioned just about everything.

As the drive continued, our conversation soon dwindled and we began to get more and more quiet. Eventually we were silent.

We were silent for the first time is 10+ hours. It was time to just enjoy each other's company while also enjoying the silence.

As we drove north, we eventually approached Beaverton. It was time for me to go home and visit my family. It was just past 5:00 am. Cassie and I said goodbye. We talked briefly after, but we never saw each other again.

I think that's ok. The memory of that drive and the friendship we created is not ruined or touched by anything that may have happened after.

I was greeted by my family and Felipe. I wanted to, but I couldn't sleep for long because I would be going to brunch with my friends. There was a catch though, I was surprising them.

A couple weeks before my visit, I had been talking to Daylynn about my trip. I decided I would surprise everyone for Blair's wedding. The surprise came the very next morning.

Daylynn had been lobbying for a brunch with everyone.
I drove my mom's car out to east Portland for our brunch. As I parked and got out, I tried my best to hide, I'm not sure how, but when I saw my friends approaching, they also saw me. My plot had been foiled.
I noticed Jared driving a car I had not seen before. He, with others in his car, turned down a side street and I followed on foot. I had recently seen Justen, but no one else. It had been 8 months since I had seen anyone else. Needless to say, I was excited to see my friends.
We eventually reached each other and shared hugs. None of them knew about the fact that I had lost my job. In the next coming days, they would.
As we went to brunch, we picked up right where we left off when I had seen them last. Conversation flowed and I received the much needed friendship I so desperately needed. Don't get me wrong, Allyssa and Ryan were helping to fill that void in Utah, however, when it comes to your best friends that you basically grew up with, nothing can compare.
Later that same day was Blair's wedding reception. Before that, I

went and visited Blair's family. I had not seen them for over a year. When they last saw me, I was getting ready to move to Salt Lake City and begin a life as a dedicated church member.

I was now faithless and in a rough patch.

To preface a bit, members of the church are married in the temple. Only those that are "Temple worthy" can enter the temple and see the wedding ceremony take place. This is referred to as "being sealed for time and all eternity."

LDS church members believe marriage is between a man and a woman. Without needing to go into detail, the church is against gay marriage. To be worthy enough to enter the temple, one must abstain from premarital sex, alcohol and coffee. One must pay their full tithe of 10 percent per pay period. Whether that is finding $10 on the ground, or your full month's salary, that is what is expected.

Blair and his wife were temple worthy while was not.

When I went to visit Blair's family, it felt like it did before- a second home. I hugged Katie, Tim and even Blair's little sister.

Tim asked me a question that I believe led to them figuring out I was drifting away from the church. Tim asked if I would be at the temple ceremony. I had to answer no. He didn't ask why. Rather than giving me a chance to explain, It seemed I was written off. I doubt this was his intention, but that was my interpretation.

Later in the day would be Blair's wedding reception. In the meantime, I went home and took a much-needed nap.

This wedding reception would be the time when I would see many members from the Oak Hills ward. Blair's family had been in the ward for as long as they can remember. They knew everyone and everyone knew them. They watched Blair and his siblings grow up, marry and have kids of their own. Now it was Blair's turn to be part of that cycle.

I was going to see church members that thought I was still active. I had decided I was just going to lie. It didn't make sense to tell them the truth. It would distract from Blair's wedding reception and would turn into church members asking me a million questions and bearing their testimony to me.

When it came time for Blair's wedding reception, I was excited and I was happy for Blair.

A couple summers before, Blair, Justen and I took a camping trip to a now popular destination in eastern Oregon called, Three pools.

While sitting around the fire, we began to speak about future goals, travel plans and even relationships. Justen posed a question to Bair. "Blair, do you want to travel more?" Blair had served his mission in Indonesia and had recently gotten back from travelling abroad and visiting Indonesia for the first time since his mission. Blair's answer was "I want too, yeah, but if I don't have someone with me, then what's the point?"

Blair had longed to be married. I was happy my friend had found the perfect woman for him. Blair's wife was basically him. If you ever meet Blair's wife, rest assured, you've met Blair. This is a good thing.

As Blair's wedding reception rolled on, I spoke with many church members. We shared memories and they asked me how I was doing. I told them "great" and "Salt Lake is wonderful." As much as I loved all these people, I couldn't confide in them because I knew what their responses were going to be.

Let's say I just told them I had lost my job. Their answer would most likely be "Well Aaron you just need to have faith in paying your tithing." or "I remember when I had no idea where my next meal would come, but I paid my tithe and food appeared in my cupboard." While those stories do exist, they never built my faith.

Let's say I said "I'm losing my faith." there answers would range from "Well, did you pray?" or "Aaron, I have found so much peace in reading my scriptures. There is a special spirit when you do that." also, "Aaron, just have faith." These answers are what you will hear church members, not just of the LDS faith, but christianity, say all the time. These answers stopped working for me. They put you in a bind that if you pray and don't receive an answer, did you not pray hard enough?

This was also an answer frequently given on the mission. Want people to teach? Have faith. I saw too many great missionaries look at what they lacked, rather than what made them great as a person because of this philosophy.

Nonetheless, I looked those church members in the eye and told them I was doing great. I stuck close to my friends for the sake of comfort. I saw Blair sparingly, and I have barely seen him since his wedding reception. Him and his wife are happily residing in Utah. I'm happy for him and I'll see him when I see him.

After the reason I came was over, it was back to the reality of my situation.

I tried to find a rideshare home, but nothing happened. Salt Lake City was proving to be a very unpopular destination. I didn't want to go back. I wanted to stay. My life was back in Salt Lake City, though.

I gave up looking for ride shares. I decided I was going to bite the bullet and fly. Last minute tickets were not cheap and I really did not want to spend the money. I was at a crossroads. Stay home and figure it out with help from friends and family? Or go back to Utah with no job, no car and questions looming about my future.

I decided to go with the latter of the two. I was not ready to give up on salt Lake City.

I ended up being back in Beaverton for 5 days. I wanted to stay because it would be easier, but at the same time I wanted to go back to my freedom in Salt Lake City, no matter how constricting my current situation was.

I found a plane ticket for $435. I took it. I didn't do much those last couple of days. Since I had surprised my friends, it was impossible to plan anything since I had surprised them. They had their lives to attend to.

I mostly pondered what I was going to do back in Salt Lake City.

I searched KSL, like I had done plenty of times before to find a car. I reached out to several people, and only one person got back to me. We decided that I would come take a look at the car when I landed back in Utah. It was eventually time to address parts of my life I wasn't ready to do.

End of summer, 2015 Chapter 8

As I bought my plane ticket I began to get ready to head back to Salt Lake City. I realized I couldn't do any of what I needed to do alone. I gave Ryan a call. I told him my predicament. This was a humbling moment for me.

Very often, I don't like to ask for help. It's just easier for me to do it myself, even if that means a hard position for myself.

However, I was out of options. I spoke candidly to Ryan and he understood. He was not only willing pick me up from the airport, but also drive me down to Highland, Utah to pick up my future car. That is about a 45 minute drive south of Salt Lake City with no traffic.

As I landed, I grabbed my bag and went to find Ryan. I walked out and began looking for Ryan.

We began driving south to Utah county. We spoke of my trip, he told me about how Utah had been treating Allyssa and him.

I had cash in hand for the car I was buying. I was buying the car for $500 and would soon find out that $500 was overpriced for this particular car.

We pulled into the neighborhood, which was in a very middle class part of town. I immediately saw the car. It was a 2002 Mazda Protege. The front passenger side window was replaced by a plexiglass cut out, that was the shape of a window. It had to be duct taped into place.

This car did not have a key. Instead, the car had a screw-driver since the key cylinder had been drilled out. My

stereo system was non-existent. In fact, my standards for a car were non-existent. I needed something that would help me just get by. I didn't care to prosper at this point, I just wanted to have my needs met.
The tire was flat, so the seller was "kind" enough to pump it up. I test drove the car and it was fine. The engine worked great, all the lights did their job. I bought the car because I was desperate. I needed a car to open up my options for a job.
I thanked Ryan for his time and what he did to help me. Ryan coming to help me would end up being a constant theme over the six months or so. Salt Lake City would have killed me if it was not for Ryan and others that helped me.
I had previously made plans for that night with a friend named Kim. These plans were on my mind as I drove back to Salt Lake City.
Kim was an interesting lady. By the end of the night, our relationship would be even more interesting than it already was.
Kim and mines plans were a bit of a taboo. At least, it would have been if I was still employed at the Covey. Us meeting under these circumstances was almost a perfect representation of our connection and the sheepish relationship we ended up having.
I met Kim several months before while working at the Covey. Monday-Friday I

worked with my manager and another leasing agent, however, on Saturdays, I worked by myself.

I loved Saturdays because I did not wear the proper uniform, I did not play appropriate music and I certainly did not keep most of the rules.

It was on one of these Saturdays that Kim walked into the office and the first thing I noticed was that she was drop dead gorgeous. She was older. She was in her mid-forties at the time. She walked into the office in her flowy black summer dress with her beautiful blonde hair moving and waving with her every move.

I was immediately enamored by the way she looked. She took a seat and the first thing she commented on was the song that I was playing. It was "Uncle John's band" by Grateful Dead. She mentioned her love for the classics and she said she was impressed by my knowledge of such.

Not that my knowledge was anything deep or intricate, but it was enough for her to take notice. She must have been in that office for 2 hours. Of course, the reason she was there was to rent an apartment. That subject would end up being a small fraction of what we talked about.

She eventually left to go grab lunch. When she came back, she signed a lease and everything. However, we kept talking and talking.

I wasn't quite sure how I felt about this. I had been feeling like I was in a lull at this time in my life. I was just kind of existing and didn't have any passions I was currently in pursuit of. Part of me wondered if Kim was somehow there to help me find these passions and served a purpose other than someone I would only lease an apartment to. She did help me feel a rejuvenation for the things I love. Eventually, we parted ways, for the time being. However, we had exchanged numbers and I felt an attraction to her. I didn't know if it was reciprocated or not, though.

She lived two buildings up from my me. We saw each other relatively regularly (1-2 times a month.) We always had little five-minute conversations that included flirting, alluding to plans being made and a lot of eye contact. One of those times, in particular, sticks out.

We ran into each other at what is called the DIY festival. This festival is held at the Gavlin center in the middle of downtown Salt Lake City. It's one of the bigger events during the summer.

I was there with a friend. I did not expect to run into her. When I did, I embarrassed myself so bad I did not think I would ever see her again. She clearly had been drinking when I saw her looking as gorgeous as ever.

She was wearing a blue romper of some sort with her dark sunglasses and wavy, blonde hair. I walked over to her and we struck up a conversation. The conversation centered on basics of how her day was going, the good to see you's and all that jazz.

My friend was by my side as this conversation was happening. As we departed, we hugged and my hand accidentally hit her drink out of her hand. To make things worse, I pulled out my wallet and refunded her her purchase of red wine. She said it was fine and it wasn't a big deal. My face must have had been bright red, because she persisted that she not accept that money. I did not think I would ever see her again, other than the occasional run-ins that were not by choice.

Even the night we were supposed to meet, I was still very confused about the situation. She was beautiful, smart and a successful psychclogist. Was she actually interested in me? Was she having feelings toward me? Was it even a romantically inclined relationship on her end? Was I overthinking the whole thing?

As I pulled into my neighborhood, parked my car and made my way back to my apartment, I did not have time to shower. I walked down to the bar. The same bar Haley and I had grabbed drinks when I drunkenly asked her to get back together with me. There was Kim,

outside in the summer heat of the night.
I joined her after I ordered a rum and coke from the bar. I anxiously made my way over to her. We greeted each other and I broke right into talking about my trip.
This is how I cope with being in a situation that I am clearly nervous about. I've gotten a lot better, but I talk a lot and really don't even break to let them talk for fear that an awkward silence will become too apparent as to ruin the night.
Our conversation went in and out of its best and worst moments. We would move closer, then further apart. My mind ran in every direction as to what the outcome might be.
I slipped further and further into inebriation.
Eventually, the server asked us if we would like the check. I noticed he combined our checks. I should not have spent that money, but I did. I paid and we left. As mentioned before, Kim lived two buildings up from me. It was a quick but uneasy walk. It was uneasy because I wasn't sure what to do next. I over thought everything about this night.
This type of pseudo plan making has backfired on me plenty of times. In a general sense, too many times have I tried to think about my next step while not fully understanding my current lot

in life. My next step used to be often very miscalculated due to anxiousness, which would render nothing close to the result I would have wanted.

I've since changed my thought process on this. I've learned it's easier to have no expectations and see what happens, than it is to possibly ruin the whole experience by thinking too much.

I've learned through trial and error that expectations are what kill perfectly good situations and relationships. Expectations can easily distract you from the moment in front of you. Of course, this is relative to the situation.

We approached her apartment and she invited me inside. We had some flirty banter and beating around the bush. It seemed to be one of those moments where both parties wanted the same outcome but neither were willing to make the first move.

Playing in the background was a Duke Ellington record. I finally decided I would rather go home than be in this situation. As I prepared to leave, she asked me a question I didn't see coming. She asked for a ride to her mother's home to pick up some of her stuff. She had recently been in a transitional period of her life. Which included moving home before she had moved to the Covey. She also had been

having car troubles. I said yes and we were off.
When we got to my car, she told me something I hadn't even thought of. She said she thought my car was stolen. The evidence became very clear to me at that point, The window was busted, keyhole drilled out and the dash smashed in, which resulted in the radio not working.
There is an episode of How I met your mother where all the members of the gang begin to call each other out on things that the other members of the group had not noticed. Once this habit, such as chewing loudly, or correcting someone in public, became common knowledge, the members of the group begin to notice this. This was that moment for me.
I had given the seller the benefit of the doubt.
As we got to her house, I witnessed a glimpse of Kim I never thought I would see. I was about to see her childhood room. I made this a bit of a big deal, internally. The reason being was that at that point, I thought I felt a connection. Whether or not that connection was going to go anywhere, even if it led to a one night stand, remained to be seen.
I walked the halls in her mother's home and followed her from room to room. She told me stories from her childhood, teens and adulthood.

We drove back to her building and once again, she invited me inside. We turned on a record and went back to our flirty, yet cautious conversation. The cycle repeated itself until I decided to leave.

We went to hug and after the long hug, we went to separate. As we did, our cheeks brushed together. As they did, I instinctively kissed her cheek and a bit of laughter erupted from her. My mind was racing. What do I do next? What do I say?

She did not kiss me back. Instead, we sat on her couch and held each other. This lasted for about half an hour. I didn't really care about the situation progressing past embracing each other on her couch. I was already content that it had gone this far. She sat up and kissed me. As we sat kissing on her couch, I became even more content.

Later we moved to her bed. The connection I had felt seemed to be confirmed. Though this feeling wasn't a connection. It was once again lust. Kim and I would be intimate once more after this occasion.

The last time I saw Kim was the night before she moved to a coastal city in Oregon. We hugged and almost forcibly, she muttered that she would like to keep in contact.

I hope she is doing well. She always discussed the wantonness to leave Utah and experience something bigger. She mentioned she had travelled all over the world, but always remained loyal to Utah. I hope she is doing great.

Though this summer was marred by so many personal challenges, there was one very bright moment. That was the day when Allyssa, Ryan, My friend white Jon floated the Weber River.

White john is an on again/off again member of my group of friends back home. In that group is my friend Black Jon. One is white, the other is black. That is how we differentiate. No negative connotation or thoughts of evident racism should be taken from this, at all.

The Weber is a short 2 hour float just east of Ogden, Utah. The float consisted of kicking off numerous rocks, dunking under logs, flipping over and lowering ourselves to clear a bridge.

Floating the river is a fun summer tradition all over the country. If you want to keep it that way, don't float the Weber.

White Jon is now engaged and I could not be happier for him. He is a great guy that serves his country in the Air Force.

While all this was going on, I was quick on the job hunt. Later that week, I had a job interview at a third party contracting agency. I had originally applied for a receptionist job, but they had different ideas.

I showed up in a button up shirt and tie because I did not realize it was a recruiting agency. I felt like an idiot. Turns out the bait and switch technique is huge when it comes to recruiting agencies.

I interviewed for the receptionist job and was told this particular job was no longer available, but they had another job that I would be an ideal candidate for. The job was a position as a ring finisher at a warehouse in the southern part of the Salt Lake valley, Draper.

I took a test that they built up to be very "make it or break it." The test was easy and I was surprised by the readiness they had to proceed in the hiring process. This should have been a red flag, but my savings were dwindling just as fast as my patience.

My next step was to interview with the actual company. I did just that and I started later that week.

One day in particular, I got ready to go to work, I was eager to continue my new job. The hourly rate was great, coworkers so far, were awesome, down to earth people just trying to make a living for their families.

The job was very hard on my hands. I remember tending to my latest scabs and cuts before I got ready for the day. We worked with small tools, large grinders and heavy sand blasters. On my third day of work, I was humbled more than at any other instance in my life.

It was a nice, warm summer morning as I walked the couple blocks to my car. My car was parked in a church parking lot about 2 blocks away. As the sun was coming up, the lights in the parking lot were still illuminated. I walked closer and closer to my car, I noticed something that instantly caused concern within me. I could not see my car's shadow that would have been cast by the light. As I walked closer, I did not see my car.

I stood there for about five minutes unable to think, move or even speak. Once I regained the ability to perform the most basic of human functions, I began to question myself. Did I park there? Did I park in this parking lot? If not, which street did I park on? If you have ever had your car stolen, then you know the emotional toll it can have on you.

It left me feeling vulnerable, humbled and like a piece of shit because as I was finally being able to stand on my own two feet, they were swept out from under me.

I had had the car for about three weeks, at this point. I immediately called my new boss and thankfully, he was very understanding. I then set out on my journey to get my car back. The journey to getting my car back, was easily one the most shitty and mentally exhausting moments of my life.

I called the police and when they did a license plate search they found that it was not registered in my name. This didn't even occur to me that it would be a problem. I didn't register the car because I wasn't working. When I finally did get a job, I couldn't afford it.

Call it ignorance, but I was more or less annoyed. The only way around that was to call the original owner and have him file the report. In the meantime, I would go and register the car in my name. At least this was the plan. There was big problem with this, I couldn't afford all the Ubers I needed to get this done, have money left to eat and register my car. I decided I needed help. I not only called, but I leaned on Ryan.

Ryan answered, listened and came to help. I couldn't thank Ryan enough. He later said something that has stuck with me. While this is not verbatim, he essentially said "Everyone has a rough time in life and everyone needs help sooner or later."

That really stuck with me. I wanted to help Allyssa and Ryan so bad but they are too self sufficient, it's not possible. The best I got was buying both drinks, every once and awhile.

We made it to the DMV and began to wait. Yes, the DMV is just as bad in Utah as it is in any other state. After about an hour, my number was called. As

I explained the situation, the clerk was more than happy to help out. She then said something that would make this situation even more difficult and complicated.

She said there was a newer title than the one I was in possession of. I said to myself "God fucking Dammit." I made a phone call to the previous owner and asked basically "WTF, MAN?!?!" He didn't even act surprised. He just said, "oh yeah, let me send that to you." What a sleazy piece of shit.

He mailed the title later that day, but that did not help me. Whatever else could be done on my end would have to wait. I asked him if he had filed the police report and he said that wasn't his problem. I very firmly told him I could not file a police report because he did not give me the latest title, so he was responsible for being involved in this situation. I felt so hopeless. Everything I currently do in life, is to never feel that hopeless again.

Once all that was said and done, there was nothing I could do. The only thing I could do that day was to head back home. I was humbled and to a certain extent, embarrassed.

I was in my apartment and remembered how before I left that day, I had dropped off rent. I thought to myself how can I get out of this situation? The only conclusion I was able to come to was to buy a new car. I couldn't sit

around and wait for the police to somehow stumble upon my car.
I decided I would have to ask for my rent money back. I was already embarrassed just by the thought of having to do so. I collected my thoughts for about 10 minutes. I recited what I was gonna say and prepared for any rebuttals. I slowly opened my apartment door and walked down the 2 flights of stairs to the office and knocked on the door.
My landlord, Lance, opened the door and I began to tell him the story of the events that had transpired that morning. Everything I had recited to myself did me no good. Somehow though, I was able to get my point across. Luckily my landlord was very understanding and handed me my rent, which I had paid in cash.
I deposited that money and refused to acknowledge what I had done, even in my own thoughts. I honestly think that was one of the lowest moments of my life. I was so embarrassed.
Someone was out driving my car while I was asking for my rent money back.
Someone was out driving my car while I was sitting in my apartment wondering how I was going to get to work.
Someone was out driving my car while I was wondering what I will be doing for food.
Before the day would end, I had the next day already planned.

The next morning I called the non-emergency number to see if there was any updates. Nope.
With Ryan's help I would be searching for a car. This wasn't going to be anything glamorous. It was going be a car that I would be buying for $600, at most. This was the type of car that you don't register or insure.
In short, it's the type car no one has any business driving except those that were as desperate as I was.
Ryan picked me up and we both agreed on one thing, Coffee. If we were going to be driving all over the valley then we would need caffeine. We were looking at several vehicles that day.
One was not too far away.
The first was in a suburb called Murray. This small city lies about 20 minutes south of downtown Salt Lake City. We would be looking at a Volvo from the 80's. Not a bus or a station wagon, but a shitty car that wasn't worth anything. I felt bad for the seller. He had this less than stellar car, that could barely run and could not get anyone to buy it. He was stuck with it.
We met the eager seller and decided to test drive the car. He had mentioned the brakes needed to be replaced. The brakes turned out to be one of the many problems with this car.
The brakes wouldn't even stop the car. There was a good chance that I could

end up in an accident while test driving the car, let alone owning it. We drove back and I politely told him no. This was after Ryan had rolled down the driver side window and the window refused to roll back up. This resulted in the owner bringing out cardboard and tape. He sat there trying to tape the opened area and asking me again if I was sure I wouldn't be buying it. I still said no.

After this car, it was off to Orem, Utah. You may remember me mentioning this city in a previous chapter. Orem is an interesting city. A lot of these cities and suburbs faced huge expansion in the seventies and therefore most homes in older suburbs are cookie cutter 1970's. The houses are runned down and lack any new remodeling. The neighborhoods take on a different feel, one could almost say it looks destitute then you remember you're in Utah county and the people are themselves, not of that stereotype. However, this does make you realize, not everything is perfect in Utah. When most people think of Utah, they think of a stepford/zion combination. Drive in the back neighborhoods and you'll realize, it's not.

Such was the case with our next stop. The car I would be test driving was a 1994 purple, dodge neon. Admittedly, before I got there, I knew things were wrong with the car. Namely, the tires.

The car needed all sorts of new interior parts, such as bushings, rods and some other important part that I don't remember.

Ryan and I hopped out and approached the house. The seller of the car was not home. Instead, we spoke with his mother. She handed us the keys and we were off. We began our test drive of the car. I did not think it was possible, but as I was driving, I easily got lost in the steering wheel. It was too unaligned, I had no idea how to even go straight.

To make matters worse, Ryan and I pulled into a church parking lot just to check lights, the engine and all that good stuff. We did not think anything of it. As I pulled out of the church parking lot, a cop pulled up behind and turned his light on. "What the fuck did I do?" While I was confused, Ryan was a bit more irritated than me. To understand this is to understand some of the previous conversations Ryan and I have had.

Ryan and I routinely had conversations that while not of the "conspiracy" nature, were often thought-provoking and riddled with questions against the "establishment."

Ryan questioned a lot of things. While he grew up in the south, he didn't have a belief in a specific god, wasn't conservative and really didn't fit any of the stereotypes of someone from the back country of Kentucky. He's not a fan of Mitch McConnell, as most people shouldn't be.

Ryan and I questioned police motives, to an extent. During this time, Michael Brown had already happened, Eric Garner happened as well as others. Ryan as well as I, do not think all cops have racist tendencies, however, we were weary.

When the cop pulled us over, I was not irritated or mad. I was just surprised.

Ryan's irritation grew. He wasn't concerned with my skepticism as to the reason why we were being pulled over. Instead, he was irritated by the lack of cause of suspicion the officer had mentioned.

The cop asked me what I was doing. I told him I was test driving a car and through his own admittance, he said we looked suspicious, but also did not say I had broken any traffic violations, or laws. He essentially wasted our time. Conservatives like to say, if you don't want cops to approach you, or pull you over, don't give them a reason. This is wrong and not always the case as to why people have interactions with the police.

Specifically speaking of cop on black shootings, too many times has the "perpetrator" done exactly what they were supposed to do and they ended up dead. Perhaps, the biggest instance of this is Philando Castile.

For those unfamiliar, here is a brief recap: Castile was pulled over by a police officer for a busted brake light. As the officer was speaking with him, he mentioned he had a weapon on him. Castile's gun was registered and he had a concealed weapons permit. Required by law he informed the officer. The officer then asked him to grab his license and registration. The officer thought he was reaching for his gun and shot him seven times. This incident was made known to the world by the fact his girlfriend, Diamond Reynolds, filmed the aftermath through Facebook live.

What was the rationale? He did everything right. He pulled his car over when the cops asked him to, he answered the police officer's questions. According to the dashcam footage, cooperated with the officer. Officer Yanez was found not guilty. If the death of Castile does not reform the Justice system, then I don't know what will.

I was white and driving a car that was not mine in Orem, Utah. I got away just fine. However, I can't help but think, if the color of my skin was different, the situation could have been different.

After the officer left, we drove back to the owners house. I did buy the car, because of how desperate I was. Driving

this car was the worst thing I think
I've ever had to do, car related.
The highway was the worst. I was afraid
to go too fast, but if I went too slow,
Utah drivers were not having it.
I made my way home with the thought,
"well, you do what you got to do." I
was humbled, but not in the sense of
bewilderment, or pity. More in the way
that things will get better and they
may suck now, but you do what you have
to do to get by.
The next day, I drove to work in that
car. I knew it was a bad idea to do so,
when I hit the on ramp to get on the
highway, I could feel my car wanting to
slip out from under me, much like if
you're driving on ice, yet it was late
august.
At this time, I was working about 12-
13, sometimes 14 hour a day. I had
never worked this much in my life, but
I got used to it.
I would work at the warehouse from 7-
3:30, then I would drive as fast as I
could to make it to my retail job. More
often than not, my shift started at
four. However, it was understood I may
be a few minutes late.
I would then work until about 8:30-9.
This schedule would last until about
november when I unexpectedly would quit
my warehouse job.
My first year in Salt Lake City was
coming to an end.

As September 29, 2015 hit, nothing unexpected happened. I didn't get any congratulatory text from family or friends. I went to work and thought about the past year.

I thought about the move to Tooele and where that led me. I thought about my old friend Matt and thought how much I could have used his friendship this past year.

I thought about Lydia, Abigail and Haley. I wondered how they were doing. Did they ever think of me? Did they ever wonder what could have happened if both parties had seen eye to eye? Did they ever hope I was doing well? I hope they did.

On this day, I thought about the church. I wondered how my life might be different had I been accepted into the ward. I thought about what might have happened if I was able to rationalize my doubts about the history of the church?

Would I be married by now?

Would I have a kid on the way?

What would my life had been like if I gave religion the benefit of the doubt?

That day I went to work, I ate my lunch, drove to my second job, went home and went to bed. I didn't post a Facebook post. I went about my life as it was at that time. I didn't express my feelings on social media, nor did I reach out to anyone to vent about the previous year.

Utah beat the shit out of me.
Utah just about destroyed me.
 that year, I learned that when life is going great, don't act like it. Keep chipping away for what it is you want. I learned more about myself that year than I did any other year. I grew more than I was anticipating. What transpired, was nothing I could have imagined before I had moved.
While in Beaverton, I thought my life in Salt Lake City would be great. Blessings and bliss? Endless. The reality of my move was not anything I was prepared for.

"Money speaks in Utah." - Robert Redford
Chapter 9

While I was working in Park City, Utah, to know one's surprise I ran into car trouble. The brakes on my beloved 1993 Nissan Pathfinder went out and it was going to cost upwards of $900 to fix. Seeing as how to I would be moving to Seattle April 20, 2017, I decided to tough it out and take the bus to work. One day I decided i would leave work early. Because of this, I accidentally got on the wrong bus. This would easily be a fear of mine in any other state, but I was not troubled by this while in Utah. I knew the valley, the transit system and if all else failed, calling an Uber or a Lyft was an option.

As I rode the bus, I put together the steps I would need to take to get home. I needed to take the bus to the Meadowbrook transit center and get on the Blue line heading to City Creek. As the bus pulled into the transit center, I began to gather my things. I made sure I had my wallet, phone and keys. I buckled my backpack on the top part by my chest. I had started doing this after watching a video of someone getting their backpack pulled off by someone from behind. It became a habit of mine to always buckle my backpack to myself for that reason. I grabbed my water bottle and made my way to the front of the bus. I distinctly remember stepping to the side and making sure I had a good song playing. It was "Don't look back in anger " by Oasis.

I began walking toward the train platform which was about 50 yards away from where we had been dropped off. As I began walking, a man that did not look homeless, beckoned for my attention. He attempted to ask me for money. This happens a solid three to five times a day when walking around downtown Salt Lake City.

Out of habit, I didn't think twice, nor did I pause my music. I kept walking as if he did not exist. Was this mean? Was this shallow? I suppose, but I was numb to having sympathy for the homeless when it came to giving them a dollar. Each person is different and each situation calls for a different response, but I feel like we're predisposed to think the homeless population has less than admirable motivations. Personally, I have/would rather donate to a charity.

As I bought my ticket, I took a seat on the platform. A lady who appeared to be just a bit older than me began walking toward me, all the while pushing a stroller. Her young child fast asleep. Groceries were dangling from the handles and they were swaying from side to side. She took a seat between me and an older gentleman. Between five seats she sat in the middle while the older gentleman and I sat on the ends.

I still had my music playing at this time. She began to rustle around within her bag of groceries. She was looking for a snack for her and her son.

The woman opened a fresh pack of strawberries. Her son, that was now awake, took a strawberry and threw in onto the train tracks. As he did this, I paused my music. I couldn't help but share a giggle with the now laughing mother and older man.

She looked at me and held out the container of strawberries. She offered me one, as well as the older gentleman. I love strawberries, but I hardly ever buy produce. As a man in my twenties, my diet mostly consisted of breakfast burritos, fast-food and oddly enough, tuna and pickle sandwiches. The sweet

taste of the fruit caused my jaw to ache.
As I ate my strawberry, the mother began to talk to both of us. She spoke of her young son making the news because he came into contact with the drug fentanyl. Luckily, her son survived but she spoke about how scared she was.
She told the story of worried mother. She spoke candidly about how she had no idea how she was going to pay all the medical bills and the problems that come with one of her problems being solved.
I got on the next train, I never saw her again. Nor did I see the older gentleman, again. As I got on the train so did the presumably homeless man that had attempted to ask me for money. We pulled into the next stop and were greeted by a large police presence.
The Salt Lake City Police department had done several of these transit sweeps that summer. The goal was to arrest those that had issued warrants. Those that were found dealing, on drugs or breaking any other crimes were given the option of treatment or jail.
The homeless man exited the train and was immediately surrounded by about 3 police officers. I couldn't make out what his predicament was, but it looked like an officer was writing a ticket for an offense that I can only assume was the absence of a purchased ticket.

As the Blue line pulls into downtown Salt Lake City and the 6-7 skyscrapers are not engulfing your view, it makes a stop at the courthouse. When it stops at the courthouse, the usual suspects hastily get on. Their reasoning, unknown. Whether they are paying a ticket, leaving jail or simply just at this stop because it's convenient, will never be known. But their bewilderment and sometimes lack of caring is evident.

As the blue line pulls into city creek I do my routine of checking my cell phone, wallet and keys. I buckle my backpack and grab my water bottle. I'm now on the last leg of my trip home. I walk the three blocks home exhausted and ready to eat dinner. It's a cold sandwich form the local grocery store, Harmons. As I lay my head down on my pillow, I think about my day. What was good, what went wrong. I watch a couple youtube videos, check all my usual apps and I begin to mentally prepare for the next day.

In the coming days I began to reflect on this moment. What I witnessed, while nothing extraordinary, is not a reality many in Utah nor those outside care to know about. Whether it's the crime rates, the homeless population or the drug epidemic that is sweeping Utah, as well as most of the country.

Utah has some of the most interesting local politics and social constructs in the country. A perfect example happened during the 2016 general election. Utah is traditionally a conservative state. The last time Utah voted democrat was in 1964, when Lyndon B. Johnson defeated Barry Goldwater in the general election. What is very revealing about this, is this is the during the midst of the civil rights movement.

At this time, Democrats were labeled as racists and bigots. However, the switch happened when republicans took a stance against segregation. When this switch happened, African-Americans began voting Democratic. This essentially turned the south into the conservative hotbed that it is today.

Republicans saw segregation as an overreach of government powers. They wanted a limited government, in this regard. So Utah voting for a democrat during the civil rights movement is a little puzzling. However, by 2016 it had been over 50 years since Utah embraced a democrat for president.

In the 2016 general election, Trump did win Utah, however, not by a large margin of victory. He won Utah with 45.5 percent of the total votes. Hillary had received 27.5 percent of the votes.

Perhaps the biggest surprise of the election, other than a terrible human being winning, was Evan Mcmullin. The third party candidate entered the race in Utah as a means to thwart Trump's hopes of winning Utah. He garnered 21.5 percent of the votes in Utah. He received more votes than any other third party candidate in a single state.

Mcmullin represents a change within Utah. Less than half the state voted Republican, which is nearly 30 percent down from the 2012 general election. Many LDS members are cold, hard republicans with deep nationalistic roots.

One can say the church implies "manifest destiny." This is the same logic that pushed westward expansion in one form or the other. This is the same logic that Joseph Smith (founder of the LDS church) used to begin his settlements with the promise that "Zion" will be built. During the early days of the church, the members were the victims of heavy persecution. This was the reason the church pushed for westward expansion.

The church holds all lobbying power within the state. LDS members make up the dominant voting base and the church yields enormous amounts of power in Utah's local domestic affairs. Reading the local news (Ksl) you will almost certainly read about the how "state lawmakers met with church officials." This leads to many problems for obvious reasons. Many of the federal, state and local representatives are members of the church.

One of those, on the federal level, was Jason Chaffetz. The former Congressman from Utah, stepped down from his position on June 30, 2017.

On february 9, 2016 Chaffetz held a town hall that had to be moved from a small, local building to Brighton High school in Cottonwood heights, Utah. The reason being, because the number of attendees was not what the Chaffetz team expected. He didn't know he was as hated as much as he was, which was evidenced by his post town-hall comments.

I am proud to say that I attended with my friend, Nina. Just like Chaffetz, we did not anticipate such a large crowd. We did not make it into the auditorium. (Though, there was about 100-200 seats chaffetz would not let be filled.) Instead, we joined the nearly 300-400 protesters outside demanding we be let in. Chaffetz truly is a piece of shit. His willingness to not hold Trump to the same level of accountability he tried to hold HRC to shows his true morals.

Every reelection cycle, Chaffetz biggest donor is Nu Skin. As aforementioned, the legalization of pyramid schemes are a reality in Utah and Nu Skin represents the worst of them.

This company all but owns Chaffetz. Nu skin had donated close to $100,000 to Chaffetz campaigns over the years.

The former congressman Chaffetz has also put in his two-cents about the then newly proclaimed national park, Bears ears in southern Utah. Following Utah politics, it is easy to come to the conclusion that the state congressman and representatives don't follow their constituents. If this was the case, I would not have been accused of being a paid protester by a former congressman of the United States of America, Jason Chaffetz.

Even when state representatives try to follow what their constituents want, it doesn't work and ends up being a waste of taxpayer money and in the following instance, it isn't actually a problem. Perhaps, the biggest example comes from State senator Todd Weiler.

I have a very weird and interesting connection to Todd weiler. While I have never met him, his son, Tyman Weiler served in my mission in Phoenix, Arizona. While he probably would not recognize me if we were in the same room, we get the same updates on facebook regarding the mission and how peers from the mission are doing. Senator Weiler was responsible for pushing forward S.C.R. 9. The opening statute of this bill states "This concurrent resolution of the Legislature and the Governor recognizes that pornography is a public health hazard leading to a broad spectrum of individual and public health impacts and societal harms."

This is very problematic because, first and foremost it's an overreach of church and state. Whether you're a Republican or democrat, this is should not be seen as okay. This is very clearly an example of the state trying to regulate morality over other more pressing issues.

How do you enforce that? Is it criminal action or a public health issue? It's an asinine law that has real consequences. When resources are pulled from other, very much needed programs to regulate what people do in the privacy of their own homes, it becomes a problem for the taxpayers.

There is a movement in Utah, specifically Utah county, called "Fight the new drug." This is the type of movement all the want-to-be cultured BYU students join. This doesn't work for me and many other residents in Utah, because why fight the new drug when the old drugs are still there. They're just as pertinent and infinitely more dangerous.

However, this bill was signed into law by Utah Governor Gary Herbert. While money does in fact speak in utah, so does the "righteous morality" of the church. This "righteous morality" only applies to certain subjects though. My personal opinion, is Governor Herbert is a waste of a person. He puts his hands in every money-making scheme in the state and in order for him to sleep with himself at night, he need to push his beliefs through politics just to think he isn't as bad-intentioned of a person that he actually is.

Meanwhile, he is actively ignoring actual problems facing the state.

Utah has a severe homeless problem that really hinders the city in terms of proper growth and expansion. A number of years ago, Salt Lake City was applauded for have a 91 percent elimination of homelessness. This number looks amazing on the surface, however, when you dive into it, it's very misleading and almost downright manipulative.

The state of Utah counts their homeless population on a single night in January, yearly. If a homeless person ends up finding a place to sleep out of view, or a couch as opposed to a park bench, they are not considered homeless by the state's standards. Utah stopped counting individuals that reside in a homeless shelter for long periods of time as homeless, as well. Even though, the next night, they may be on the streets, they won't be considered homeless.

The flawed numbers brought attention to Utah and they were seen as a pillar of excellence when dealing with the homeless population. It was heralded as such an achievement that the god himself, Jon Stewart, sent one of the daily show correspondents, Hasan Minhaj to investigate.

The then director of Utah's Homelessness Task force, Todd Pendleton, stated "We have reduced our Chronic homelessness by 72 percent since 2005." This was just the beginning of the inflated reality. Later in the year, the director of Utah Division of Community and Housing, Gordon Walker, threw out the number of 91 percent drop in chronic homelessness. The number 91 was what began Utah's ascension into being a false example.

When Utah began a new method of counting, that was when the number dropped. If the facts are misguided and false, that really hurts the homeless and the state. Those numbers are what help create proper funding for programs.

In late 2016, it was announced the long used and consistently overcrowded Road home in downtown Salt Lake City would be closing its doors. This was a problem because it would displace a large portion of the city's homeless and leave them without much needed resources.

The mayor of Salt Lake City is Jackie Biskupski. In 1998, Biskupski was elected to the Utah house of representatives, becoming Utah's first openly gay person elected to public office. She tried her best to choose new sites, but was almost always met with opposition. Perhaps, the biggest show of opposition to helping the homeless has already happened.

On March 26, 2017, Draper (City in the southeast corner of the Salt Lake Valley,) was the site of an open house where the city was to discuss the two proposed homeless shelters that would come to the city. The announcement of these shelters had come the day before. The opposition was comparable to the Chaffetz the town hall meeting, only on the other side of the political spectrum. At one point, a homeless man that was brought in to speak, was booed off stage by the crowd.

The open house was held two miles away from the Draper Temple. Draper is 75 percent LDS. Exactly 1 week later during general conference, the church announced that they will be building five new temples. Utah, as well as Draper, cheered with excitement that temples will continue to be built in Colombia, Chile and the Democratic Republic of the Congo. Many of these places need more humanitarian aid than a building many won't be able to enter. Matthew 8:20 reads " And Jesus saith unto him, The foxes have holes, and the birds of the air *have* nests; but the Son of man hath not where to lay *his* head."

These church members profess to love and worship, but cannot seem to understand that Jesus was presumably homeless while he lived his 33 years. This scripture is the definition of homelessness. For Draper to celebrate their temple and others around the world, but deny those that have not a place to lay their head is not a practice of Christianity. It's called being an awful human being and not having compassion, or basic human decency to take care of those that need help.

The scary part of all of this is the overarching mentality of the members of the government that are LDS. They are very clearly using their powers to influence those that are not LDS. When a state senator can propose a bill about porn and get it passed, but a bill regarding Utah's homelessness can't get enough support, the church has too much bearing on the state.
The breach of church and state go all the way back to the time Utah was first settled. Though, against Utah's wishes, they were not admitted to the union when they first petitioned to the United States government. Brigham Young, the church's second president and prophet, was technically the governor of the Utah territory when

the United States gained control of the land after the Mexican- American war.

Of course, back when Brigham Young was the territorial governor, he never imagined the problems facing Utah today and if he did, he did an inadequate job of preparing church members, state laws and policies for problems that their faith cannot address.

Brigham Young did not see the opioid problem facing Utah.

There is a certain cognitive dissonance to the opioid problem. Many Utahns shutter at the thought of a homeless person that is addicted to heroin being in their neighborhoods, cities and even places like their grocery stores.

Yet, when it's a functioning member of society that is also a member of the church that lives in the suburbs, it's a sad story because of where they are at in life. It's sad because they have shown they has more to their life and is willfully throwing it away. People have seen what they are capable of.

I'm the same way, though I try not to be when looking at a homeless person, but it's hard to see their potential as it relates to their drug addiction. However, that homeless person, if given the right treatment, is just as capable of living an ordinary life just as easily as that suburban mother or father. Both are sad, but generally speaking, only one will provoke empathy from many members of the church.

This had always intrigued me. When does the story switch from sad, to no mercy? In Utah, your sympathy is relative to your status and temporal looks.

In 2014, (at the time of writing, in early 2016, the numbers for 2015 were not yet finalized.) Utah ranked 7th in drug related deaths in the country. The private citizens of Utah have often blamed this problem on the homeless. They sit in their modest middle class suburban homes, read their newspapers, watch their news and draw their conclusions based on what they see, not what they choose to ignore.

Utah has some of the highest ACA enrollment rates, per capita, in the country. The homeless are not enrolled in the ACA. The homeless are not the ones walking into a doctors office trying to convince them of pain so egregious that only prescription drugs can cure the problem.

Granted, this is not all inclusive. There are homeless addicted to opioids that are enrolled in the ACA, but just as easy as it is for a homeless person to get heroin, it's just as easy for a suburban middle class man, woman or teenager to get prescription drugs.

This creates a certain ignorance in the fact that the state does not want to confront this problem because it would shatter the perception that Utah isn't the Zion they were promised by the previous generations. The problem begins with confrontation and the Utah bubble is very much to blame for the lack, thereof.

It's easier to place blame on a problem like homelessness because no one person truly knows a solution. When you blame a problem on a solution that cannot be fixed, it's easier to put it on the back burner and ignore it.

This past election cycle there has been a minority that is not ignoring the problems such as drug addiction and homelessness that hold the state back.

Salt Lake City has traditionally been a blue dot in a red state. Though the blue is relative to the state, comment still stands.

I personally have attended a number of protests in Salt Lake City. This shakes the rest of the state. This perpetuates an unwanted sense that

Utah isn't as perfect as once thought by the LDS majority.

Conservatism works for the majority of Utah because by nature, the majority are subservient to both the church and the government. The LDS church, itself, teaches very patriotic (borderline nationalist) principles.

The majority of Utahns have a belief in God and that serves as their motivation for their thoughts and decisions. Though many hypocrisies abound, on both sides, that is the truth.

When something happens that doesn't have an answer, many that are religious are quick to either thank God, or proclaim a higher knowledge and logic that is above theirs and ours understanding that God is responsible for this current situation or predicament

This creates a culture of a subservient population. Why ask questions when there is an ominous being watching over us that knows everything past, present and future? I should clarify, this is subservient to their beliefs. The stubbornness is easy to see when it comes to progressive ideologies that do not necessarily affect the person in any way, shape or form.

A perfect example is planned parenthood. In the year 2016, planned parenthood of Utah had 88,707 clinical operations. Abortions made up 2,015 of those operations. That is 2.27 percent. That 2 percent is enough for people to figuratively pick up their pitchforks and demand justice for the "murder of babies." Nevermind the other 97.73 percent of total operations.

Subservient nature enters into this category because it is a long held belief that each person is brought to earth because they have a purpose. There are two reasons for such a distaste for planned parenthood. One is political. The other is a for all intents and purposes, a religious crusade.

The political reason is because the republican party loves to cut any program that people can rely on for help. Welfare, Meals on Wheels, CHIP and of course, the ACA have all come under a huge amount of scrutiny from the republican party, not just in Utah, but nationwide. Planned parenthood falls into that category. The emphasis on planned parenthood, which includes a heavily doctored footage of a "fetus sale" and outright attacks from the Fox news network are religiously pushed.

The religious zealots of the republican party only seem to care that the baby is born and demand that it is self sufficient and not seeking handouts. Christianity is very clear about the shedding of innocent blood and in the eyes of a faithful Christian, it does not get more innocent than a baby, until they need assistance from the government
Being subservient to Christian values is being subservient to conservative principles. They are too intermingled and entwined to undo. Accepting change does not fit into that mold. Utah especially, has a very hard time accepting the idea that the state is more diverse than their political and religious philosophy can handle.
A subservient nature is rooted deep into the history of the Utah. However, to understand this behavior, one needs to look back at Joseph Smith.
As it is well documented, Joseph Smith was a known polygamist. even though it is well recorded, his first wife, Emma Smith, was in denial of such practices. This subservient nature of the church is clear to see in some of the early letters between church officials.
Benjamin F. Johnson was one of Joseph smith's private secretaries. As a result of this, he knew Smith better

than most people. Johnson penned a note in which the date is unclear, however, this note was sent and received by George S. Gibbs. At the time, Gibbs was presumably serving as secretary to the First Presidency of the church. The letter was in regards to the early stages of the practice of polygamy.

A quote from this letter strikes me as odd. I'll save you any doubts and questions I may have, but let's, like many Utahns assume, the practice of plural marriage was ordained of god. Smith relayed a story to Johnson. The story, regarding polygamy, states "Joseph was commanded to take more wives and he waited until an angel with a drawn sword stood before him and declared that if he longer delayed that command he would slay him. This was the manner brother Hyrum (Joseph Smith's brother.) teaching to me, which I then did not need, as I was fully converted." This story shows that smith had reluctance, but was ultimately willing to oblige to the commandment of polygamy. It also shows, Johnson didn't even need the story because he was already converted.

As present-day Utah was settled, the men were taught that whether they wanted to partake of polygamy or not, it was a commandment. Submissive behavior is such a huge part of Utah politics because the church relies on an accountability system that is based on self-discipline.

When Utah first wanted to join the Union as far back as 1851, the Federal government told them they had to drop the practice of polygamy. It took nearly 40 years, scores of church officials in prison, as well as in hiding, before the church changed their stance and were allowed to join the Union on January 4, 1896. The stubbornness and willingness to go to jail, not join the country and continue practicing polygamy shows the submissive nature. Only the behavior was to appease God, not a government that was in its infancy. The practice is done away with and Utah is currently the 45th state to be admitted to the union. The same logic and ideology that drove the church to follow polygamy, also drives many members to have the same feelings toward abortion, gay marriage, drug rehabilitation and even global warming.

In the church, you are taught not to give into the world and remain heaven-bound. This is reflected on many archaic beliefs that do not serve anyone that is not LDS. This is why non-separation of church and state is so dangerous in Utah.

Utahn's consider themselves very patriotic. The republican party claims to have a love for America and by doing so, an almost monopoly-like claim to the country's true form of patriotism.

The pillars of this patriotism are supporting the military, law enforcement and as of late, the president. Supporting the president only applies to republican presidents. But to be fair, I don't support trump and I make a small claim to be patriotic.

The republican party has adopted this notion that "if you aren't with us, you're against us." Little do they realize, it's possible to support Black Lives Matter while not wishing death upon police officers.

It's possible to support the military but not the actions of war and it is easily possible to love this country without supporting Trump.

The nationalistic principles the church instills began before the church was even founded. A now deceased member of the quorum of the twelve apostles, Elder L. Tom Perry, gave a speech at BYU in February, 1976 confirming this very notion. The talk itself, while very well written, gives a very revealing insight into the way LDS members, as well as christians, view themselves in America. The talk was a celebration of sorts. It was the bicentennial of the United States of America.

The beginning of the talk speaks about the early leaders of the church expressing concern over the future of America. Perry Quotes Brigham Young, who in turn, is Quoting Joseph Smith, " "Will the Constitution be destroyed? No: It will be held inviolate by this people" ; and, as Joseph Smith said, "The time will come when the destiny of this nation will hang upon a single thread. At that critical juncture, this people will step forth and save it from the threatened destruction. It will be so."

Even early on, LDS members, whom at this time, the majority came from Christian backgrounds, (Methodist, Baptist and Catholic) are being groomed and taught that they will inevitably be the true patriots. The seeds were being sewn for a dichotomy that is being felt today, more than ever.

For further evidence of this, all you need to do is read this speech a little bit further. President John Taylor, who served as the church's third president and prophet makes an even more divisive claim, "When the

people have torn to shreds the Constitution of the United States the Elders of Israel will be found holding it up to the nations of the earth and proclaiming liberty and equal rights to all men, and extending the hand of fellowship to the oppressed of all nations. This is part of the program." Taylor does not separate religion and equal rights. He binds them. On the surface, these comments are eloquent and read well, but this changes the definition as well as standards of liberty and equal rights. He is declaring that those who are religious and righteous, truly understand and deserve liberty and equal rights.
"Washington, Franklin, Jefferson and others "gave praise to god" for their wisdom" is mentioned.
The speech goes on to speak of the constitution having endured longer than any other in the world. Because of the longevity is must be God's will that such a document has lived on.
Joseph smith once stated "The constitution of the United States is a glorious standard; it is founded in the wisdom of god. It is a heavenly banner." It's beliefs like this that drive the church, as well as the republican form of patriotism. While

my examples are meant to show the connection between the LDS church and Utah to patriotism and conservatism, the ideology spreads to all the majority of conservatism.

"In summary, I have attempted to again remind you of *your* responsibility to preserve the righteousness of the land of America." Perry states as he begins his conclusion of the subject.

LDS members and republicans alike, have taken it upon themselves to save the constitution. They feel that since they have a claim on patriotism, they, and only they, can interpret the constitution correctly. The sense of patriotism is ingrained deep into most LDS members. The church very much views itself as the last line of defense between a desolate land once called America and the fullness of the gospel, which cannot happen without America as defined by the constitution.

This sense of patriotism has led to an alienation of progressive principles as well as those that believe in them.

In my personal opinion, this divide that had been growing and grew exponentially under the Obama presidency and hit full steam with the election of trump. With his election, political division came to a head. It was solidified when republican Majority speaker, Mitch Mcconnell went "nuclear" to confirm Neil Gorsuch. He eliminated the need for a super majority (60) and instead changed the rules so the senate only needed 51 votes.

While I won't spend a lot of time on national politics, this is detrimental to a democracy and will serve as the day the Mitch Mcconnell killed bi-partisanship in the senate. This need to protect republican principles that do not allow progression, are ignorant at best. Yes, this country was founded on conservative and republican principles, but it cannot be sustained on those ideals.

The thought of non-separation of church and state run so deep in Utah, that the cities geography was shaped because of it.

The very fundamentals of Salt Lake City were built by the church, for the church and for the church members. The layout of Salt Lake City comes from Brigham Young, who received his inspiration from Joseph Smith. Smith penned a letter called "City of Zion." Though This letter does contain a couple different modifications made by Young, for the most part, it is intact in its fullness.

Perhaps the most notable feature is the wide streets. The average Salt Lake city street is 132 feet wide. This definitely has its faults. Early in the book, I mentioned when my friend Justen came to town. We ended up at a bar, but the original plan was to grab some food. The distance between us and my favorite pizza shop (Pie Hole) was technically five blocks. Half-way through the walk, they wanted to give up and go to a bar.

This shows how unwalkable Salt Lake is. Granted, there are pockets like Sugarhouse, Main street and Ninth and Ninth, but for the most part, it is a hard city to get around in. This has a negative effect on the businesses downtown.

Without a walkable city, it makes it hard to grow and sustain local businesses other than the necessities such as grocery stores, gas stations, etc.

State street is the probably the busiest street that runs through downtown Salt Lake City, it is also one of the widest. Because of this, it is the main entrance and exit into town. There are sections that include state and federal government buildings. There is a very small section that includes a pizza shop and several bars. However, the further you go, the only businesses are motels that are used by the homeless and closed down shops that only take up space.

If Salt Lake City is to continue to grow it'll need to adjust the grid system and strive to become a more walker-friendly city. The grid system spreads the city out and makes it too difficult to even talk to your neighbor across the street.

However, the true change Utah needs is a social one. Religion has infected Utah politics since its inception as a territory as well as a state. The distribution of population plays into the states culture, as well.

Most Utahns reside on the wasatch front. 5 of the state's major universities reside there, as well. Weber State University, University of Utah, Westminster University, Utah Valley University and, of course, BYU.

The distinction between Utah and Salt Lake county are largely made by looking at the diversity of opinions by those enrolled at the universities in each county. BYU and UVU both represent Utah county, almost to a T. Perhaps, that is why Utah county has been culturally unchanged for generations. These two universities feed into the culture and local economy. Yes, many members leave the state, but a good portion do not. They stay and continue to add to the many problems that impede on anyone that is not LDS.

The polarizing nature is one that hurts Utah in many ways. With Salt Lake being the state's capital, it creates a certain paradox. The state legislature dictates the state, and by consequence, the state's capital. Those legislating do not represent a large minority of progressives. Those that do represent those districts that differ in religious beliefs are progressive/liberal, in nature. They are easily drowned out by the overwhelmingly republican utah government.

This is what leads to pornography and shutting down planned parenthood, being priorities over the homeless population and opioid problem.

Utah is a state that is pretty much all over the place. Too many people are not represented properly, while others are represented too well. It has as many problems as it does successes.

Utah is a beautiful state. The politics are murky at best and in my opinion, have a long way to go.

September 30, 2015 to September 29, 2017
Chapter 10

The morning of September 30, 2015 was not any different from any normal day at that moment of my life. It was a Wednesday, which meant work.

Something was changing, though. I was growing tired of my job.

My full-time job was still at the ring manufacturing warehouse. Everyday my hands underwent bleeding, cracked skin and deep cuts. Not a day went by that I didn't have some new cut or a scab being ripped open. My manager was younger than me and definitely had a power complex.

I couldn't stand it. One day in particular in late November cemented my decision.

I came to work and was selecting the music I would be listening to while I worked. Let's call my manager Betty. Miss Betty walked over and proceeds to talk sternly to me about a problem that I did not create, nor that I had been involved in and was not able to solve. Once I told her this, she left. She came back about five minutes later and spoke of the same issue. I repeated myself. She eventually came back about 10 minutes later. While I was changing my playlist, she snapped "NO PHONES!" I had had enough. Call it immature, or childish, but this was it for me.

Whether I was justified or not, I decided to quit right then.
20 minutes passed and after consulting with members of my team, I walked up to her and quit. This didn't play out like I thought it would. The building was controlled by a fob. The fob was used to get both in and out of the building. I handed her my fob as I quit. She had to escort me out of the building because the door was across the building. Worst way to quit, ever.
While all this was going on, I had signed a freelance agreement with SLUG magazine as a contributor.
In Salt Lake City, I got my first taste of music journalism. This became and has continued to be my passion. The reason I mention this, is because I had finally found my true passion- Music Journalism. Anything that did not support or bring me closer to a career with music journalism, seemed like a waste of time.
Eventually, I would take a job at a call center. Those type of jobs really are as bad as everyone says. I worked for a government contractor that was the hotline for the Affordable Care Act. I learned a lot about the ACA, which was great in a couple of ways. I was able to truly learn all about this bill. I learned about how non-controversial it should be. However, I also learned how bias people can be. Too many times, people on the phone

would use that as a soapbox to tell me their political beliefs.

The overall ignorance of some people is too great for people to ever come around and understand. I learned about the flaws, but I also learned about what makes it great. Many people used the phone line as their soapbox to tell you about how much they hated this law and the president that had his name on it. By contrast, the phone lines were also used by single mothers, the elderly and people from all walks of life that were happy to even have healthcare.

I talked to single mothers that were simply speechless that they were able now to finally afford their medication after years of making sacrifices to provide for their children. I talked to the elderly that relied on the ACA for their hospice care.

During the time I was at this job, my car situation was not the best. I had bought a car that was simply, only good enough for getting from point A to point B. It's important to note, I definitely broke the law when it came to these cars. I never registered them, nor did I insure them.

I knew I was breaking the law and the risks involved, but what was a broke kid to do? I didn't blame anyone else, but me. I saw myself in a hole and it was time to dig myself out.

I relished in this. To me, when life get rough and you can't even stand up, that's when it really doesn't matter what you do. Granted, human decency and the law are still important things to remember, but your ability to pull yourself up by whatever means, shows the true character of your person.
As time went on, I lost more and more of my soul working at the call center. I saved up money and eventually decided my first action was to buy a new car. One that I would register and hopefully keep for a long time.
That decision was in the background until one morning, it became a need. I was required to work 14 days in a row. This didn't bother me at all. That would be 2 full days of overtime, which meant working through the weekend. This would have been fine, if I wasn't oblivious to the parking rules at the church parking lot near my house. I came home like it was any other Saturday night. The next morning, my car had been towed. When I parked my car the night before, it was the last time I would ever see that car. Since the car was not registered in my name, I couldn't even grab my stuff from my car. It was gone.
I did not dwell on this too much. There was no point. It was very black and white. Luckily I got my paycheck with all sorts of bonuses and overtime. I

used nearly all of this money to buy that new car.

I did some searching, and I found the car I wanted. A 1993 Nissan Pathfinder. I awoke one morning to Ryan picking me up. We drove down to the suburb Murray. This is truly a Deja vu' story. This had happened so many times. This would be the last time, though. We test drove the car and I fell in love. Granted, it needed work, but I was willing to take care of that. If it meant having a semi-stable car, I'll take it.

I bought the car that I would later name "Liza Jane" after listening to the Nina Simone version. Ryan and I went and smoked the first and last cigarettes in that car.

That car would end up costing me close to $2,000 in repairs. While it was a burden at time, paying that money, if you've ever driven a Nissan Pathfinder, I think you'll understand.

While I bought the car, I had quit my job at the call center. That job was nothing more than a quick paycheck. The reason being, because I wanted to leave Salt Lake City for a while. Not move away, just take a break, reset myself, then come back. Salt Lake had beaten the shit out of me and it was time for something new. Not permanent, just an escape. I decided to work on a cruise ship.

I took a job with American Cruise Lines. The reason I tell you the name is so you don't make the same mistake I did. There were things I absolutely came to love, but if I had the opportunity to do it again, I wouldn't. I was still working at Uptown cheapskate throughout all this. Even when I quit the call center job, with about a month before I left, I worked the retail job. On my last day, my co workers, which included Ryan, bought me a cake. I truly felt grateful for Ryan and Uptown Cheapskate. I was going to miss Utah, but it was time for a break. The plan was to drive home to Portland, then I would fly out to New Orleans for training. I drove home and spent time with friends and family before I would embark on this journey.

I flew to New Orleans and did my training on a beautiful paddle-wheel boat. After that, I learned I would be working on a boat called the Independence. This particular ship was located on the east coast. Through the 3 months I worked on this ship, We would sailed as far south as Fernandina Beach, Florida, all the way up to Portland, Maine.

When I first got to the ship, All my coworkers were strangers and I had a hard time adjusting to the long hours and all the small detail-oriented tasks.

One story I do wish to share, was the night two other coworkers and I went out in Fernandina Beach. It was my friend Ivy's birthday. Ivy and I, to this day, are still very good friends. The other was Mike, who I still speak with, occasionally.

I can't remember the reasoning, but no one else came out. Perhaps, the biggest rule on the cruise ship, was no drinking, on or off the ship. The reason being, if there is an emergency, we cannot respond intoxicated. This was a rule broken by everyone, including the managers. You just didn't talk about it. Culturally speaking, It was don't ask, don't tell, type of policy.

We proceeded to the clubs. Which, is as weird as everything I had ever heard about Florida. We all got incredibly drunk. So drunk in fact, we all made it back to the boat, past curfew, all at separate times.

The next morning was turn around. Which meant that the previous week's guests leave, and the new patrons come on. We had two hours to get the boat flipped. I have never been so hung over in my life. That day was a struggle for me. I found out it was even harder for Ivy. Still to this day, we don't know how, but Ivy had fallen and got mud all up and down her leg. This was not discovered until halfway through turn-around.

It is stories like this, with the people I love, that make life worth living. Our jobs sucked. We worked 12+ hours a day, seven days a week, for 3-4 months. However, I could not have done it without the bond I came to have with those people.

We made stops in cities like Savannah, Georgia, Charleston, South Carolina, Baltimore, Maryland and even Providence, Rhode Island. We also made stops in small cities like Brunswick, Georgia, Beaufort, South Carolina, St. Michael's, and Crisfield, Maryland and even Nantucket, Massachusetts.

One of the most tender moments of my life happened with these strangers turned family. For the first six weeks of working on this cruise ship, we sailed one itinerary. This was from Fernandina Beach up to Charleston. We made weekly stops in Savannah. Savannah was the highlight of that itinerary. I loved that city then and I still love it. Once again, we were working 12+ hours a day, seven days a week. We were exhausted and Savannah represented an escape.

Not all the stewards were 21 but we all had a common denominator and that was a love for drinking as to a means to relieve ourselves our thoughts of work. In Savannah, you are allowed to drink alcohol on the streets and in the squares, if you have the alcohol in a cup.

Often times we would buy our cheap beer, with our red cups and drink the night away in one of the squares.

We would dance to Runaround Sue, then minutes later, sing Matchbox Twenty. We were loud, obnoxious and I loved every minute of it. As time went on, our group began to split up. People went home, got promoted or were let go. Truly an amazing experience.

When it was finally my turn to go, which happened suddenly and unexpected, it shook me. I was not ready to leave. I was not okay with leaving my new-found family. It happened though. It was time to go back to regular life. I flew from Portland, Maine to Portland, Oregon. It was time to go back to Salt Lake City.

As I flew back to Portland, I wasn't sure what to do. I wasn't sure how long I'd still be in Salt Lake City, whether I was going to move to another city, or back home to Portland.

I decided to go back to Utah. I had been paying rent on my apartment while I was on the east coast, because I loved that apartment. I drove back in June, with no A/C. The drive was awful. Specially through Idaho.

I was back in SLC for a week when I accepted a job at a resort in the mountain town of Park City, Utah. It was nothing glamorous. I was a manager in the housekeeping department. That job was interesting.

Many people like to say foreigners are taking the jobs of many hard working Americans, I call bullshit. I was one

of 5-6 native english speakers in a department of about 70-75. The majority of the housekeepers were refugees.
They hailed from Iraq, Sierra Leone, Chad and later we would have an influx of H2B housekeepers from Jamaica. I only recall seeing one white housekeeper there, once.
It's nothing more than a political talking point.
When I came back to Salt Lake City, I decided to rededicate myself to writing. I applied for an internship I had no business getting. The internship was for a content writing position. I did end up filling their vacancy. I was one of about 8 content writers.
This internship was really one of the most important turning points of my life. I made friends that'll last a lifetime and skills that are currently carrying me into my career.
Though, there were things I disagreed with. We were assigned 15-20 writing pieces a week. These ranged from 300-400 words for about 5-6 different clients. This was done for a flat fee of $500, which was not collected until the end of the internship, contingent on finishing all assigned pieces.
This turned into a part-time job minus the working wage. Often times, I would work my full-time job, then go straight to a cafe and begin writing. I would work out my schedule of pieces that needed to be done that day and often

times I wouldn't reach it. I would eventually get my work done, but it was always a struggle.

A flat fee of $500, in hindsight, simply was not worth it. I learned a lot, don't get me wrong, however, I did roughly 420-500 pieces while I was there and that averages out to about $1 a piece. This company definitely took advantage of their interns.

Nonetheless, when my internship was over, I collected my check and even applied for a job, which I did not get. This confused me. I fit in well, I was even one of only two interns to finish my all my assignments. I legitimately believe it was because they had interns lining up that can do the work for a measly $500 check.

The people I worked with became close friends. It was so nice and refreshing to be around those that felt the same and were passionate about writing.

It was during this internship, I thought that I could be content with staying in Salt Lake City for a long time.

It was also during my internship my car was stolen for a third time.

I walked out for work one morning to the same parking lot my car had been stolen from 2 times before. I did the same thing before, wherein I stood still, in disbelief. Called my work, called the police. This time was a bit different, though.

It was too routine for me to be especially anxious. I went back to my apartment and went back to sleep. I took the day off from work.

As for work, I took up public transportation. This was October/November, 2016 so it was easily one of the worst experiences I had, given the cold. The next morning I walked to the bus stop in the worst rain storm Salt Lake City had seen in months. My mental state sent me to a place of wishing the worst upon the person that had stolen my car. However, I decided later that morning, while on the bus, fuck it. I'm over being mad. I'm over being depressed about it. It wasn't going to bother me anymore. The worst part of my time in Salt Lake City was over and it was time to change my mindset to best reflect that.

This city had already beaten the shit out of and got the best of me several times. Not this time. I decided to roll with it. I decided I wouldn't waste my mental well-being on a car that I most likely would not be getting back.

About 3 weeks later, I received a phone call from the Salt Lake City police department. They had found my car. It was found in the last place I would have thought. Behind Westminster University.

Westminster is known for being a very wealthy school with very wealthy students. This confused me. After a desperate phone call to Ryan, we made our way to Sugarhouse to pick up my car. This would be the last time I would make this type of phone call to Ryan.

After much more money and time, my car was back and running. After my internship had ended, the holidays passed and the thick of winter had approached and passed. I was finally in a "what now" mindset.

One night Alyssa, Ryan, I and our group of Utah friends, that had grafted us in, were at our favorite bar. Johnny's on second. Ryan had spoken softly but sternly that him and Allyssa, were 75 percent sure they would be moving to Los Angeles.

Allyssa and Ryan's semi-made declaration got me thinking. If Ryan and Allyssa moved, who would I have? I had several other friends that I was close with, but Allyssa and Ryan were my first true friends in this state. They mentioned they were ready to move on to bigger and better things. I agreed with them that they should move on.

This is what got the ball rolling with my thoughts. If they were ready to move on, why wasn't I? Well, I had begun thinking about moving as early as the fall of 2016, but never took it seriously, until they had made their mind up about moving.

My parents had moved from Portland, Oregon to Seattle, Washington in August, 2016. So that was an option for an easy way out and frankly, into a new and exponentially more progressive and exciting city. I conceded that I was ready to leave. The reason I moved to this city was no longer a presence in my life.
Allyssa and Ryan moving was all the push I needed to leave. When they finally decided they were moving for sure, I decided on the very same thing. Allyssa and Ryan were my first, true natural friends in Utah. Their friendship and Utah became synonymous with each other. I couldn't live in Utah without them. It just wasn't an option.
My last few months in Salt Lake City were very strange. I didn't realize how much I loved Salt Lake City and didn't realize how much I would miss this city.
I remember walking in the bitter cold, one night with my headphones in and realizing how grateful I was for my car being stolen 3 times. Having multiple heart breaks and just as many moves.
I was thankful for my new friends and the support system they gave me.
I was thankful for the church being the reason I came, but not the reason I fell in love with this city.
I was thankful for all my different jobs and the many people I met. Most of

all, I was thankful for all the lessons I had learned.
I thought about my life and the direction I wanted to take.
I thought about the mistakes I made and came to the conclusion that they were necessary.
I thought about the things that went right and the thing that wrong. As I thought about leaving Salt Lake City, I thought about what it taught me and what this city inspired me to do with my life.
One day on my way home from work, which included a 45 minute bus ride, "I and Love and you" by The Avett Brothers came on my shuffle. I had heard this song a million times over before.
It seemed as if this was the first time I listened to this song. I was leaving Salt Lake City with a new frame of reference, New belief system and new career goals. "Brooklyn, Brooklyn take me in" took on a new meaning. I substituted Brooklyn with Seattle. Rather than get excited about Seattle, at that moment. I Thought about the shape I was in. I thought about my previous two and a half years.
I bawled like a baby thinking about leaving the Salt Lake valley. I was scared, but excited at the same time. I was moving on from the most difficult time of my life. In those moments though, it did not seem like the most difficult, instead, it felt like I had

already lived the best time of my life. I never felt more alive than I did walking the hallowed and sacred streets of Salt Lake City.

I decided I would be moving April 20, 2017. This was purely coincidental, I swear. Allyssa and Ryan were moving April 18, 2017. I helped them move and it was as bittersweet as can be expected.

Our good friend Alex was there to help us. It was a weird feeling. It was an end of a very pivotal time in my life, but it didn't feel like it.

After we were done loading up the U-haul, they would be one step closer driving to their new life in Los Angeles. We had shared many laughs and great times in one of our favorite restaurants-spitz. We were accompanied by Allyssa's mother, whom I had met previously at thanksgiving.

We enjoyed our lunch while conversing about our past memories. The meal ended and we embraced each other and that was it. They were off the next day, I was off two days later. It was a change that I didn't feel ready for. Though, it was going to happen, regardless.

Most big changes in your life are instantaneous, whether it's a friend proposing to his future wife, your car being stolen, or being laid off from your job

For me, I had to watch my closest friends in Utah move, put in my two

weeks at work, pack and eventually drive 13 hours to Seattle.
Allyssa and Ryan are in Los Angeles, while I'm in Seattle. They seem to feel more at home than they ever did in Salt Lake City. They love it and I am happy for them. While our contact ebbs and flows with time, I know that when we see eachother again, it'll be a sweet reunion.
On April 20, 2017 I made my way to Seattle. I rented a car because my car had died about a month before.
I arrived in Seattle eager and excited to be back in the Pacific Northwest. I was finally back home.
At the moment of writing this chapter, I am currently a social media specialist at a hardware installation company. I play music, write and seek to be the best person that my trials in Salt Lake City taught me to be.
During my last year and a half in Salt Lake City, I made a decision when it came to the church that changed things still felt to this day.
As mentioned before, I had stopped going to church in June of 2015. I decided to stop going because I just couldn't believe in the church anymore. I had read facts about the history from reputable sources, not what is referred to as "Anti-Mormon" literature.
Too many things did not add up, too many inconsistencies to reconcile. I lost my "faith." In reality, I gained

another understanding, free of an accountability system that did not allow me become the person I wanted to be.

In November, 2015 the church's stance on children of LGBT parents became even more public than it already was. The policy reads:

"Children of a Parent Living in a Same-Gender Relationship

A natural or adopted child of a parent living in a same-gender relationship, whether the couple is married or cohabiting, may not receive a name and a blessing.

A natural or adopted child of a parent living in a same-gender relationship, whether the couple is married or cohabiting, may be baptized and confirmed, ordained, or recommended for missionary service only as follows:

A mission president or a stake president may request approval from the Office of the First Presidency to baptize and confirm, ordain, or recommend missionary service for a child of a parent who has lived or is living in a same-gender relationship when he is satisfied by personal interviews that both of the following requirements are met:

1. The child accepts and is committed

to live the teachings and
doctrine of the Church, and
specifically disavows the practice of
same-gender cohabitation and marriage.

2. The child is of legal age and does
not live with a parent who has
lived or currently lives in a same-
gender cohabitation relationship
or marriage."

As a convert, I found this appalling.
Essentially, if you are a child of LGBT
parents, you can only be baptized into
the Church of Jesus Christ of Latter-
Day Saints if you have permission from
the most senior members of the church,
or simply be 18 or live on your own.
As aforementioned, one of the church's
main points of doctrine is free agency.
The ability to choose for yourself.
This is frustrated by this policy.
This angered me and helped me realize
how the church truly views the LGBTQ
community. We read in the book of
James; "For whosoever shall keep the
whole law, and yet offend in one point,
he is guilty of all."

Why are children of the LGBT couples
given different treatment? According to
this verse, parents of the different
sexes that beat their children, drink
excessively and commit adultery, are
one of the same. Yet, the church is
giving preference to those whose
parents are of the same sex.

I felt betrayed. I had spent two years preaching a gospel that was supposedly filled with love and acceptance. Almost 3 years later, here I was, pissed and hurt that the same church would single out those whose parents have made a choice they may or may not support.

I disagreed so much to the point, I had to take action. I spoke directly and candidly with a friend of mine that has served in the same mission as me. He left his mission early and had not been to church longer than I hadn't. Him and I made plans to go out drinking that friday.

A Facebook invite went out for a mass resignation. The location was Beer Bar. My friend and I made our way down and signed all the applicable paperwork. To be honest, I didn't really think anything would come of it. I thought it was more symbolic than anything else. This was not the only mass resignation of members of the church. More than 2,000+ individuals hand delivered their resignation papers to church headquarters themselves.

This was it. This was the result of moving to Salt Lake City. I had moved to Salt Lake City hoping to be an active member of the church and eventually raise a family in the LDS faith. Yet, here I was drinking a beer, right after I had signed the papers that would remove my name from the church that I had committed 6 years of my life to.

My name had been on the records of the church from July, 2009 to November, 2015. For 6.5 years, I had committed myself to a higher level of accountability than others, which admittedly, I did not always reach.

I had entered the waters of baptism and gone through the LDS temple ceremony. I had accepted and made promises that had an eternal bond, only to have them undone by drinks of alcohol, bowls of weed and promiscuity.

The deterioration of my accountability happened because I was growing into myself. I joined the church as a 17-year-old who was not sure about who they were and had no idea who the person was that they wanted to be or would eventually become.

The church is the church. They have their standards and there is no compromise when it comes to being a member of the church. Many members will tell you, I failed to live up to the standards I promised to. I don't see it this way. You can't live up to something you don't want to, nor can you fail when you never really tried.

I left the church because I realized the person I was growing into, was not meant to be held accountable to the abstinence to things such as drinking, smoking, sex before marriage and believing LGBT people are equal in every way, shape or form.

For me, the church didn't work. I grew away from the church and am happy I did. There was no sustaining myself in the church once I began to harbor thoughts that were not in line with the church.

For some, religion works. It truly does. For those people, that is great. I am a huge believer that it does not work for everyone because not everyone can be held to certain accountability standards. However, If religion and a belief in the traditional Christian God and Jesus Christ edifies you as a person and pushes you to be a better person, pursue that believe to the fullest extent until you are the best person you can be.

Our goal as people, should be to uplift and edify our fellow brothers and sisters. This does not have to be done by handing someone a bible, church pamphlet or saying a prayer for them. This can be done by listening to them about their day, supporting them in their latest endeavors, or as Ryan did, helping someone who is having car troubles.

Form September 29, 2014 to September 29, 2015 I had the shit kicked out of me by a city I came to love. I had experiences that taught me lessons that I still learn from. I met friends that

are lifelong and lovers I'll never talk to again.
I entered the Salt Lake Valley as a member of the church of Jesus Christ of Latter-Day Saints.
I lost my religion in the Mecca of the west. I expected to gain everything that God had to offer me.
I served my mission and busted my ass, only to find out that my conviction would not last forever.
My morals as a person have not changed. I still believe in the good of humanity. I have seen NFL players and owners unite against a racist and mentally unstable president.
I've watched private citizens use their boat to save lives in the aftermath of a hurricane.
I've seen lawyer's work free of charge to help refugees from Iraq leave their homes for the American dream.
Perhaps the most inspirational, happened shortly after Valentine's day, 2018. After a shooting at a high school in Parkland, Florida, watching high schoolers, who's first major news story of remembrance was presumably the shooting at Sandy Hook, take on the NRA, president Trump and gun laws, brings me such happiness and hope for the future.
My opinions and views on the church vary. I don't have anything against the church. I left out of anger, but I have since calmed down about the situation.

The church does do a lot of good in the world. They have an amazing humanitarian department that is always at the forefront of natural disasters. I do sometimes find myself angry about the hypocrisies I experienced as well as other arbitrary issues.

Toward the end of my time in Salt Lake City, I did an interview with "Humans of Salt Lake City." Here is my interview in its fullness.

"I'm from Portland, Oregon. When I came home from my mission to Phoenix, Arizona, I went out with some friends and they started ordering drinks and I joined them. I had a drink and I smoked some weed. I'd grown up doing that anyway and just stopped when I converted. I got caught up in a cycle. During the week, I might drink or smoke and then, on Saturday, I was on my knees repenting and taking the sacrament on Sunday. I went to Elder's Quorum and did everything I was supposed to. I'd have six solid months and then I'd lapse for four. It all coincided with bouts of depression.

I went to church regularly even though I was drinking and smoking. I went to a mutual activity and hoped to see someone I knew. I sat at a table by myself and not one soul made any attempt to talk to me. I tried to talk to people there but I felt embarrassed and ashamed. I decided not to go to church for a while and to see if anyone noticed my absence.

In November of 2015, I had my records removed from the church because I just couldn't reconcile myself to the decision not to let children of LGBT members be baptized. At first, I really regretted it because I know that coming back takes a long time. As time went on, I started to open up and told one of my best mission buddies that I was no longer active and that I'd had my records removed. He's still a good friend but there are those that behave as though I don't exist anymore. Our commonality is gone.

I love Salt Lake City but I'm getting ready to move to Seattle. I've spent time wondering now what I should be doing with my life. I'm going to miss being close to Temple Square and those feelings I had when I joined the church. I think, when I move to Seattle, any last connection to the church will be gone and I've thought a lot about what could have been. It's going to be different. I gave it my best and I'll always remember it in a positive light, but I think that what I believe to be right in the treatment of people is valid and worthy of consideration, too."

I feel this interview does an adequate job at capturing my thoughts about leaving Salt Lake City.

Though, I do wish to make a single correction. "I'm going to miss being close to Temple Square and those feelings I had when I joined the church." I don't miss any feelings because those feelings were artificial. Created out of an excitement of something new, not a holy spirit or anything otherworldly.

The final part of moving to Seattle is true. Once I left Salt Lake City, any connection I had to the church was essentially done. This was the first time since I was 17 that the church was not prevalent in my life. Even after I left the church, the temple was less than a block away. In Salt Lake City, the 2nd or 3rd question when you meet someone new is "are you mormon?" It's inescapable.

For the first time since July 18, 2009, I did not have to worry about being asked or presumed to be LDS. It's not on the mind of people not in Utah.

The latter part mentions my thoughts on what could have happened. I still have those thoughts. What would have happened if I stayed active?

What would have happened if I lived the principles and following of the church? What would have happened if I had met an LDS girl I instantly clicked with and got married?

Would I be happy?
Would I get so far, only to realize I had made a mistake?
I don't know.
September 29, 2017 was spent like many other nights. A date with a woman I met on tinder. She was smart, funny and beautiful. It didn't go anywhere.
I've learned life repeats itself over and over. Whether it's verbatim, or just a vague resemblance, situations transpire that feel familiar. This is why our own personal history is so important. Being able to look back at the lessons we've learned and apply that to our current situation in life is what makes it so deeply personal and vitally important.
To my friends in Salt Lake City, I love you and thank you for everything. Thank you for supporting me in everything I ever did.
I will never regret my time in Salt Lake City. I can't. I won't. Salt Lake beat the shit out of me and I wouldn't have it any other way. The lessons I learned when I could not afford to eat, pay my bills or even get gas, were worth it. The person I was then was not prepared. The person I was could not have been ready. The person I am today is not possible if it weren't for the ill-prepared person I was and the experiences I had.
Thank you Salt Lake City. I will always love you.

Made in the USA
Middletown, DE
21 April 2018